DRAGO'S

*Love,
Klara*

DRAGO'S
An American Journey

By Peter Finney Jr.
Foreword by Mike Rodrigue

PELICAN PUBLISHING
New Orleans

Copyright © 2024
By Drago's Foundation
All rights reserved

The word "Pelican" and the depiction of a pelican are trademarks of Arcadia Publishing Company Inc. and are registered in the U.S. Patent and Trademark Office.

ISBN 9781455627868

Photographs courtesy of the Cvitanovich family

Printed in the United States of America
Published by Pelican Publishing
New Orleans, LA
www.pelicanpub.com

*To my wife Carolyn, who likes her oysters only one way—
charbroiled—and who usually eats just five, leaving seven for me.
That's an equation for a happy marriage.*

Contents

	Foreword	9
1	Bread for the Journey	15
2	The Silent March	21
3	Nothing Is Beautiful Under Communism	35
4	A Man of Letters	43
5	Mardi Gras Romance	49
6	Special Delivery	54
7	Gut Check	64
8	"We Did a Good Thing"	72
9	After a Lifetime of Preparation, Instant Success	78
10	Back of the House	85
11	Majoring in "Daddy"	92
12	A Mother's Love	96
13	Mom and Pop	106
14	"Star Was Born"	113
15	Tommy Gets His Spurs	125
16	The Croatian King	132
17	The Shirt	146
18	Baby Steps	150

19	Katrina: "A Moral Obligation"	162
20	Spreading the Love	173
21	Paying It Forward	180
22	"Hey, Mr. Tommy"	192
23	"Make My Day"	199
24	"Living the American Dream"	208
	Index	219

Foreword

Why would the Cvitanovich family, which opened Drago's Seafood Restaurant in Metairie in the 1970s, ask the owner of Acme Oyster House, probably its biggest competitor, to write the foreword for "Drago's: An American Journey"?

The answer to that question has everything to do with the Cvitanoviches' DNA.

I am humbled to introduce you to the authentic "American journey" of Klara and Drago Cvitanovich and their two sons, Tommy and Gerry, especially because their example of hard work, perseverance, and humanitarian service is a teachable moment for an America that seems to be experiencing more than its share of distrust, discord, and division these days.

I didn't meet Tommy Cvitanovich until the 1990s, but as a kid growing up in the Lakeview area of New Orleans in the '60s, I was vaguely familiar with his parents, Drago and Klara Cvitanovich.

The original Drago's Restaurant at 789 Harrison Avenue in New Orleans was the go-to place in New Orleans for fried shrimp, and, for me, fried shrimp was the holy grail of New Orleans food. My dad would always let us order first, and I remember him looking at me as I always ordered shrimp. That was my Friday night treat! I'm sure fried shrimp was one of the most expensive items on the menu. I think the "look" my dad gave me came as he was adjusting his own order to make sure he had enough cash in his pocket to pay the bill. Those are some great memories.

It wasn't until much later that I learned Drago Cvitanovich didn't own that restaurant. It was owned by his sister Gloria and her husband, Drago Batinich. Drago Cvitanovich was the imposing "brother-in-law" with the wide smile and the enormous hands who shucked oysters and tended bar just inside the entrance. His eyes were always sparkling.

As I got older, I began to hear extraordinary stories about how Klara and Drago went out on their own to start their own mom-and-pop restaurant. To this day, it never ceases to amaze me how a couple from Croatia could immigrate to the United States with no money—and with Drago knowing almost no English—to forge a seafood restaurant empire that today is known throughout the world.

Ultimately, success comes down to hard work, and that's what Drago and Klara exhibited, night after night, week after week, in creating their version of the American dream. The Croatian American work ethic they instilled in their sons, Tommy and Gerry, was fundamental. Tommy and Gerry absorbed by osmosis the truth that success was no accident.

Drago and Klara came to this country after World War II, fleeing a regime that suffocated any dreams of personal achievement. I love the subtitle of this book—"An American Journey"—because Drago's and Klara's stories are an example of what America can provide for individuals who seize the opportunity in front of them.

Whenever you walk into their restaurant in Metairie, a Cvitanovich is there, minding the store. They get it. They walk through the dining room and actually listen to their customers. With all the familiar faces, there's a real comfort in that. You have entered their home, and, of course, their home is your home.

Restaurants are notorious for their revolving-door staff. Drago's waiters, cooks, expediters, bussers and managers have all been there for years. That's a testament to how much emphasis Drago and Klara placed on taking care of their employees. They know how vital staff members have been to their success, and they reciprocate that loyalty. I don't know of many restaurants that have paid their staff members when natural disasters (hurricanes, oil spills, or pandemics) have forced the restaurant to shut its doors. Drago's does and will.

Hurricane Katrina in 2005 was the watershed moment for New Orleans, and it told you everything you needed to know about the Cvitanovich family. Just days after the city was swallowed up, they were at the front lines in Metairie and New Orleans, serving a total of 77,000 free hot lunches to people who were trying to piece their lives together again.

I'm proud to say that the New Orleans hospitality industry is unlike any other in the United States for the extent to which we rally together for all kinds of charitable and humanitarian causes. What Drago's did after Katrina by feeding thousands of first responders and returning residents—through the simple act of serving people a warm meal—won't ever be forgotten.

And, believe me, in New Orleans, we have long memories.

Finally, Tommy's creation of the charbroiled oyster is probably the most significant, one-bite, grand slam in New Orleans food in our current generation. As an ode to Tommy's "charbroiled" oyster, we at Acme serve the "chargrilled" oyster. No matter what you call it, it's our number one seller, too. I try to needle Tommy, "You invented it; we just made it better!"

Nearly every restaurant in the country that serves oysters tries to emulate Tommy's creation. Imitation is the sincerest form of flattery.

Some young people today have the mindset that they should be instant financial successes and make money quickly. As Klara and Drago proved more than sixty years ago when they arrived unpretentiously by train in New Orleans, you simply don't get in the way of Croatians chasing the American dream.

All it took was hard work.

Mike Rodrigue
owner, Acme Oyster House

DRAGO'S

1
Bread for the Journey

Klara Buconic, a native of Stupa, Yugoslavia, was just eighteen in 1957 when she stood on the deck of the *Queen Mary*, gazing west at the gray nothingness of the Atlantic Ocean.

Klara's dream of new life and freedom in America—particularly aspirational after the ravages of World War II and suffocating, post-war Communist rule—seemed not to matter. The Atlantic salt peppered her face, and she wasn't so sure of anything now.

Klara's father Stjepan, who before the war had been a successful and deeply respected, self-made entrepreneur, had saved enough money to buy the eldest of his three daughters a steerage ticket on the *Queen Mary,* leaving Cherbourg, France, in August 1957 for the five-and-a-half-day passage to New York, where Klara would be united with her aunt.

Stjepan had seen massive changes in his country of birth. Yugoslavia was formed after World War I through a merger of territories of the former Austro-Hungarian Empire, which included Croatia, with the Kingdom of Serbia. After World War II, a Communist government under Josip Broz Tito was established, a seminal event in the life of the Buconic family.

After the war, all the material success Stjepan had worked for was seized by Tito's Communist regime.

"My dad's goal was that I was going to get out of the country, no two ways about it," Klara recalled. "That was his goal, and it eventually became my goal."

Finally, the goal was in reach. Untethered, the *Queen Mary* was steaming west toward America.

Everything seemed to be going well on the day of her departure. Klara squeezed into the low-fare cabin with five other girls she didn't know, but for some reason, she couldn't share their youthful giddiness as the *Queen Mary* pulled out, away from the only life she had known.

"I wanted to go to America when I left home, but when I came on the boat, I was very much down," Klara recalled. "The other girls were laughing and joking and having fun, but I felt like crying. I was looking at the water, and I was so sad. I was wishing I could go back, but it was too late. If it was closer, I would have jumped off and swum back home. It hit me all of a sudden that I was going into something so far away and so hard."

A few days later, the sight of the Statue of Liberty—a beacon to every immigrant to the U.S.—and her aunt's family's warm reception buoyed Klara's spirits. In many ways, Klara's persistence and determination in facing and conquering the unknown became a metaphor for the life she would eventually share with another Croatian immigrant—Drago Cvitanovich—who like Klara, had left everything behind to one day forge a restaurant empire founded on hard work and tunnel vision.

And, just as Klara had peered deeply into the water at eighteen, pondering her uncertain future, Klara's and Drago's life together was forever tied to water—in all of its creative and destructive power. Water nurtured life and provided the seedbed of their livelihood—and water nearly swallowed up the city that had nurtured and validated their success.

Even now, so many years after Hurricane Katrina, the eight-foot bronze statue of St. Dominic, his right hand raised skyward and his left hand clutching a prayer book and a rosary to his waist, bears the scars of one of the greatest natural disasters and engineering failures in the history of the United States.

When the levees burst on the New Orleans side of the Seventeenth Street Canal in August 2005, saltwater and God knows what else cascaded into a topographically challenged city and then percolated like a toxic brew for two weeks, swallowing everything in its gravity-driven path and creating a petri dish of poison and pain.

From Lakeview to the Lower Ninth Ward, Katrina turned a great

American city silent, dark, and desperate. Approximately 200,000 homes in the Greater New Orleans area either were destroyed or severely damaged.

What Katrina's winds couldn't destroy, the uncorked water—with no place to escape—eagerly finished off.

Even today, the watermark etched by Katrina on the statue of St. Dominic at the main southern entrance to St. Dominic Catholic Church on Harrison Avenue is clearly visible on the saint's upper chest. Since the statue sits on a four-foot granite pedestal, Katrina's water level at that spot in Lakeview measured more than eight feet.

Four weeks after the storm, Drago Cvitanovich, then eighty-three, sat in a spider-style folding chair in the shadow of St. Dominic, the church where the Croatian immigrant and his wife Klara first had brought their family to worship when they arrived in New Orleans from Canada in 1961 with three suitcases, two boys (Tommy and Gerry), and a pocketful of dreams.

In the four decades that followed, Drago's and Klara's journey of shared sacrifice, relentless work, and business savvy transformed a comfy, mom-and-pop seafood and Yugoslavian restaurant in Metairie into one of the New Orleans area's most successful eating establishments, laying the groundwork for a burgeoning empire of Drago's restaurants across the Gulf South.

Drago and Klara did it in large measure on the strength of a signature dish—charbroiled oysters—that was dreamed up one day in the eighties by their son Tommy as a garlic-butter-and-cheese-lathered alternative to eating raw oysters. A health scare, now remedied, had nearly crushed the oyster business in south Louisiana and almost cost the Cvitanoviches their original restaurant.

And now, in October 2005, all of New Orleans was crushed, looking for any glimmer of hope.

Actually, in those somber days, every New Orleanian was looking for food for their journey—something Drago could supply.

As Drago peered out from beneath the bill of his traditional be-bop cap, so popular with Croatians, he spotted a line of old neighbors and hordes of strangers queuing up in front of St. Dominic Church for a free meal served out of the restaurant's normal delivery truck. Drago's had started serving free meals to first responders and the general public in front of their Metairie restaurant on the Wednesday after Katrina before shifting in October to New Orleans. The move into New Orleans came just four weeks after Katrina, a time when residents who had begun returning home were sifting through the remains of their lives and hauling their refrigerators, mattresses, and photographs to the curb.

They had no other place to get a hot meal. There were no fast-food places or grocery stores open within miles.

That caravan of need transported Drago and Klara decades back in time.

During World War II and in the years that followed—when first the Germans and later the Communists seized control of their proud nation—food was in such short supply in Yugoslavia that bread was a treasured commodity.

One of Klara's most vivid childhood WWII memories is of young man nicknamed Spenja, who worked at her father Stjepan's grain mill before the war, secretly dropping off two loaves of freshly baked bread every Sunday to the Buconic family at the second-floor bathroom window of their home in Dubrovnik. Spenja, who after WWII was working at a Dubrovnik bakery, was simply trying to repay Klara's dad for his kindness to him in the years before the war.

"That was the treat of the week, and I never forgot this," Klara said. "So, when I see hungry people, I have to help, because I know the feeling."

Even though Klara and Drago did not know each other in their youth, Drago carried with him a similar brush with hunger during WWII, which he would carry with him the rest of his life. Before obtaining an American visa that allowed his family to immigrate to New Orleans in 1961, Drago and Klara were living in British Columbia on a Canadian visa. Drago was the head waiter at a lumber camp 140 miles north of Vancouver run by a Scottish company that was constructing a hydroelectric dam on the Frazer River.

The camp's massive dining room fed 1,200 people per shift, and the Scots in charge of the dining operations were experts in keeping the Croatian waiters and dishwashers in their place.

One of Drago's jobs was to sweep the floor after dinner.

"It's funny," Klara said. "At the end of the night, when he saw a piece of bread on the floor, he just couldn't sweep it up—he would bend over and pick it up. He would just put it away gently rather than sweep it with the broom. He became the laughingstock of everybody working there."

At night in their claustrophobic trailer home in the woods, Drago confided his real motivations to Klara.

"I didn't have bread, sometimes for six months, during the war," he told her. "I cannot sweep it. It is a sin for me."

In October 2005, in front of St. Dominic Church, Drago was beginning to show some signs of age. He sat quietly by the statue and monitored the food distribution operation, run with military-style precision by Tommy, who describes himself as being "obsessive" about "a plate never going backwards" because that slows down the delivery process.

While Klara, Tommy, and a load of Drago's employees packed the chicken pasta into clamshell boxes and placed the meals into grateful, outstretched hands, two women spotted the family patriarch sitting in his chair and shrieked: "Drago! Drago!"

"I put everybody to work but me!" Drago replied, smiling and pointing to his family, kitchen manager Freddie McKnight, and Drago's managers David Gelpi, Ivana Popich, and Vera Occhipinti.

The Harrison Avenue location of Drago's "Katrina soup kitchen" was emotionally remarkable for another family reason. Forty-four years earlier—in 1961—Drago's first job in New Orleans was working as an oyster shucker and bartender for his older sister Gloria and her husband, Drago Batinich, at the original Drago's Restaurant at 789 Harrison Avenue.

The two Dragos were not blood relatives. "Drago" is a common Croatian name and is considered a term of endearment because it means "precious" or "dear one." As the affable man behind the bar who kept the drinks flowing and the raw oysters shimmering in their shells, Drago Cvitanovich was known by the customers and employees of the original Drago's as "Brother-in-Law."

Drago always thought he and Klara would have the opportunity someday to buy the family restaurant from his sister, but it didn't happen, which Klara describes as the most difficult professional disappointment of her husband's life.

For the first time in her life, Klara saw Drago cry.

But Croatians are tough people with broad shoulders.

And, on that day in October 2005, Drago Cvitanovich was feeding hungry people with the food that his hard work and indomitable spirit had provided.

The spot where Drago sat in his folding chair—in the shadow of St. Dominic and the statue's scarred water line—was exactly sixty-five steps from the front door of the old family restaurant.

Drago was giving people their bread.

2
The Silent March

Even today, the thunder, lightning, and fire—the sounds and smells of war—are etched deeply inside Klara Buconic Cvitanovich.

The eldest of Stjepan and Marija Buconic's three daughters grew up in Stupa, Yugoslavia, a postage-stamp village of nineteen homes located thirty-five miles northwest of Dubrovnik, just inland from the Adriatic Sea.

Klara was born in 1939, Nada in 1941, and Mira in 1943.

Growing up as a child of WWII was a daily laboratory in perseverance, resilience, and faith.

Early on, German soldiers commandeered her family's three-story home in Stupa. The house was shared by two branches of the Buconic family—the family of Klara's grandfather Peter and the family of Peter's brother. The first floor was used to dry potatoes—but the Germans needed the ready-made accommodations and squeezed the families into a small part of the house.

For a base of operations, the soldiers also annexed Stjepan's grain mill and general store in the nearby village of Ošlje.

Stjepan had some formal education, going to school through the eighth grade, but he had intelligence and an entrepreneurial passion that enabled him to excel as a provider for his family and a natural leader for his community.

"My father was brilliant," Klara said. "He was like the guru of the area, and he was never scared to educate people. The entire village was proud of Stjepan."

Stjepan's father Peter was another incredibly hard worker—a subsistence farmer who grew wheat, corn, collard greens, Swiss chard, carrots, and onions and also cured Dalmatian hams.

In 1950, Klara was eleven, Nada was nine, and Mira was seven.

Stjepan had worked dutifully on his father's farm, but he wanted more for himself and his young family. That entrepreneurial streak became his calling card in Stupa. His hard work allowed him to finance and build a general store, which included the village bar, and a grain mill, where his workers would grind wheat and corn. The multi-level building allowed ample space for dried sage—in three levels of quality—to be brought in from the field by peasants and placed for sale. He was the ultimate middleman. Because it sometimes took hours for the farmers' wheat and corn to be milled and weighed, Stjepan knew they would be hungry and thirsty while waiting for their cash, so he opened a small bar that offered food and drink.

While the takeover of the family home and the seizure of Stjepan's mill in the early 1940s was humiliating, Klara remembers German soldiers being mostly cordial to her and her sisters and cousins in the beginning, when there was no active fighting.

"The Germans cooked barley and speck (cured smoked pork) in front of the house," Klara recalls. "We always saw the German guns, but they treated us okay and didn't destroy anything in the village. They were nice to us kids and also to the young ladies. The only thing I got upset about was when they gave my little sister and my first cousin, who were born three hours apart, bigger pieces of chocolate than I got in the daily ration!"

Klara's parents—Marija and Stjepan Buconic—around the time of their wedding in 1938.

But there were few games to let kids be kids.

"There was nothing," Klara says. "We did jumping jacks. We played with a rope. We played a little soccer."

Two early incidents stand out amid Klara's wartime experience. The first came after the family received word that Stjepan and his entire family might be targets because of accusations he was collaborating with Yugoslavian partisans resisting the German occupation.

"We left our house in the middle of the night," Klara said. "Everybody was nervous—running and hiding, and here and there you heard shooting. We had to hide overnight in the mountains behind Stupa. After going to the hills, we returned the next morning and cannons were shooting at us from a distance. Thank God we were lying on the ground, and we weren't killed."

Klara's most vivid brush with death came in 1943. Once again, word had come down that the Germans were targeting Stjepan for his partisan leanings.

"We heard they were coming to get Stjepan Buconic's family and were going to cut the throats of every single being," Klara said.

Instinctively, Stjepan decided he needed to find a more permanent hiding place for his wife and young children. They fled from the family home in the middle of the night.

"The shooting was tremendous," Klara recalls. "It was raining, lightning. Just horrible."

The Buconic family headed in the dark from Stupa to the coast, with only Stjepan's father Peter remaining behind ("No one was going to kick *him* out of *his* house," Klara says). At the shore, they jumped into a small rowboat and paddled a half-mile to the Island of Life (Otočić Života).

"We had taken a lot of sugar with us from the house because we knew there was nothing to eat on the island," Klara says. "A couple of the sacks of sugar got wet and turned red and got as hard as rocks from the bauxite in the ground. We still ate it, and my grandmother put it in her coffee."

Finally, in 1943, the Germans resolved to turn up the heat on Stjepan. On charges of aiding the partisans, Stjepan was jailed in Trebinje, about fifteen miles from Dubrovnik. The incarceration was brief because Stjepan had the benefit of an excellent attorney. His

Klara's grandfather Peter Buconic proudly wore his traditional Croatian garb. During WWII, Peter remained back at the family home in Stupa despite threats on his life.

first cousin Antun, who had gone to school in Austria and spoke fluent German, secured his release within a few days. As a man of letters but with no children himself, Antun also impressed upon Stjepan the value of ensuring that his three daughters were well educated.

But, in 1945, with German capitulation looming, no one was thinking much about school. Chaos continued to reign.

As the Germans fled the Kingdom of Yugoslavia, they implemented a scorched-earth policy. The Germans had used Stjepan's multi-story mill in Ošlje as a headquarters and makeshift hospital for injured soldiers. As they pulled out of the area, they torched the mill.

"The story has it they burned some of the wounded soldiers who couldn't travel," Klara says. "It was like they said, 'We can't have this building, so you're not going to have it.' That building burned for three days. You could smell the sage from miles away. My father was so upset that they thought he was going to commit suicide. He had worked all his life for it, and now it was up in flames."

The maelstrom of post-war life also pushed Stjepan to consider doing something to better shelter his eldest daughter Klara, then turning seven. He decided to send Klara to live for three years with her maternal Aunt Katie, a teacher in Podgora, about sixty-five miles northwest of Dubrovnik on the Adriatic coast.

"My mom had a heart problem, and my aunt was single," says Klara, who recalls having to move again in short order when her aunt got married and moved inland to devastated Dragljane on the other side of the mountains.

"That was the saddest thing you could see," Klara said. "Everything in the area had been burned by the Germans."

In the poverty and destruction, Klara clung even more passionately to her studies.

"I was determined to do well, plus, I had the pressure from my father," she said. "He was very strict about education. He always regretted the fact that he didn't speak a foreign language because whenever he traveled to Czechoslovakia to buy crystal for someone, he always had to hire an interpreter, and he felt the interpreter was not translating correctly. He wanted us girls to know many languages."

Beyond pursuing her academic goals, Klara also was deeply moved by the catechism instruction she received from a Mount Carmel nun, Sister Natalina, who prepared her for her First Communion at age seven.

"Little Sister Natalina, I will never, ever forget her," Klara said, smiling. "Every time I wake up, even to this day, I think of her. She had this little, bitty, really sweet voice. All I remember—and I've lived with this idea through all of my life—is the image she gave me of Jesus. She told us, 'Jesus stretched out his arms to hug you; he tilted his head to kiss you; and he was on the cross because he loved you.' I go to church every Sunday, but I feel it is more important to live the Catholic religion than to just go to church."

In 1946, the local Communist leaders of Yugoslavia approached Stjepan in Dubrovnik and said they would loan him the money to rebuild his mill and general store in Ošlje so that it could be put back into commerce.

"My father got the loan, but at the end of the work, he didn't have enough money to finish it properly," Klara recalls. "So, he used whatever money he had to finish the building."

In this case, Stjepan's entrepreneurial spirit and his ability to put up some of his own funds to finish the construction made him, from the Communists' point of view, a "person of interest."

Everyone in the tiny village of Stupa had heard the story of Stjepan's fairy tale marriage proposal to Marija in 1938. A centuries-old Croatian engagement custom is for the prospective groom to present his future bride with an *obiljezje*, a piece of fruit, usually a red apple, in which the engagement ring and one gold coin are pressed into the fruit. If the woman accepts the fruit, she is saying yes to the marriage proposal.

When Stjepan went to Marija's family to ask for her hand in marriage, the apple he presented to Marija was adorned not only with the ring but with twenty napoleon gold coins as well.

"My mom came from a well-known, wealthy family, who ran a successful dress and material store in Ston, and my dad was trying to impress her," Klara said. "This probably was his downfall later on because the whole village knew the story of how Marija Buconic had received the twenty gold coins."

In other words, Stjepan had to be sitting on a pile of money.

One day in 1948, at five o'clock in the morning, secret police officers burst into their Dubrovnik home.

Klara's grandfather Peter, seated, on the wedding day of his son Peter and daughter-in-law Marija.

"They wanted to investigate what we had in the house," Klara said. "They were looking for more gold. We didn't have any, but they put so much fear in us. My mother and father were shaking."

A few days later, a goldsmith who ran a jewelry and watch repair shop nearby suffered the same indignity. Secret police swarmed his house and began breaking through the stone foundation in the basement, where they uncovered some hidden gold.

"In one day, they put in jail the ten wealthiest people in Dubrovnik," Klara said.

"One of the jailed goldsmiths eventually broke under the relentless investigative tactics to which he was submitted," Klara said.

"They tortured him in jail so much that everywhere he had hidden the gold, he told them," Klara recalled. "One of the brothers had a girlfriend who lived forty miles away, and some gold was hidden at the bottom of some of her flowerpots. They went to her home and went directly to the third flowerpot, the fifth flowerpot and so on — they had the exact description of where to find the gold."

For six months, Stjepan remained incarcerated and was cut off from any contact with his wife and three daughters. The jail was close to the Adriatic, but the high wall ringing the old city of Dubrovnik prevented prisoners from getting a glimpse of the glistening sea. However, the Dubrovnik wall simultaneously provided an excellent vantage point from which Klara and her younger sisters could peer into the prison courtyard when their father was allowed out of his cell to take a brief afternoon walk.

"Fortunately, we knew a lady from Ošlje who had an elevated house on the wall across the street from the jail," Klara said. "She was called a 'keeper of the wall' because she was in charge of keeping the area at the top of the wall in good condition. We kids would go to her house on the wall at two o'clock in the afternoon because we knew we could look down and see our father walking in the prison courtyard. We could look at him and wave, but we couldn't talk to him."

One day, word filtered down that Stjepan and several other inmates would be escorted by guards from the jail to the courthouse for their official trials.

"They walked them down the main street like soldiers," Klara said. "The men were not allowed to look in any direction. If they looked to the side, one of the guards would yell at them. It was the first time I had seen my father in six months. We yelled for him, and when we did, the policemen would come and say, 'Stop!' My mom wasn't there. She wasn't strong enough to do that. We were allowed into the court, but we didn't understand what was going on."

Each prisoner received a perfunctory verdict. Stjepan was sentenced to a year of hard labor, with six months credited for the time he had already served in the Dubrovnik prison. He was transferred to the Lepoglava prison labor camp in Serbia, which served as an internment facility for Communist dissidents.

Just as the Germans had done in 1945 when they burned Stjepan's business to the ground, the Communist leaders made sure they punished the entrepreneur where it would hurt him the most: they confiscated his mill in Ošlje and seized the family home in Dubrovnik, which he had built in 1936.

"They said the family could stay in the house as long as they lived, but after they died, it would belong to 'everybody,'" Klara said. "Those were tough days for my mom and for the kids. My grandfather Peter supplied food for us from the farm in Stupa—collard greens, potatoes, olive oil. Whatever they had on the farm, we had in Dubrovnik."

While Klara and her sisters spent their summers and their winter vacation on their grandfather's farm in Stupa, they lived most of the year at the family home on the western side of the medieval walled city of Dubrovnik. The Buconic family house was just a stone's throw from Fort Lovrijenac (the fort of St. Lawrence), an imposing outpost perched on a one-hundred-foot-high cliff above the Adriatic Sea that is known as "Dubrovnik's Gibraltar." Fort Lovrijenac was immortalized as King's Landing in *Game of Thrones*.

The famous inscription carved into the stone above the door leading to the fortress doubled as a signpost for Klara's life: *"Non Bene Pro Toto Libertas Venditur Auro"* ("Freedom cannot be sold for all the gold of the world").

Klara was attached to the farm country in Stupa—so different from the walled city of Dubrovnik.

"I was acquainted with killing the pigs and goats and putting them up to be dried in a smokehouse, which also served as the kitchen," she recalled.

On a visit in the summer of 2022 to the family farm in Stupa and to the original site of Stjepan's general store in Ošlje, Klara had the opportunity to show her eight grandchildren the family home and store. The general store in Ošlje, burned by the Germans, now has no windows and no roof. The trip back in time created emotional flashbacks.

"I think it opened my grandchildren's eyes to the hard living," Klara said. "I told them about my grandparents, my uncle and the villagers of Stupa. There were only nineteen homes, and I knew everyone by name. It made such an impression on me. It was very important in building me into what I am today."

With Stjepan jailed, the family lived frugally in Dubrovnik. In order to make extra income, Marija took in vacationers during the summer, which meant the girls had to rearrange their sleeping quarters. The kitchen became their bedroom: Little Mira, the youngest, slept on the kitchen table; Nada (Maric), her middle sister, slept under the table; and Klara found a spot on the floor.

Klara struck a beautiful teenage pose on the shores of the Adriatic Sea.

"We even used to sleep in the attic," said Nada, who lives in Dubrovnik today. "My grandfather made wooden stairs that were transportable, but they were very heavy. There was a little hole in the ceiling, and you had to climb up there and jump through the hole. It was so hot during the summer, but that's what we had to do. None of our money was spent on traveling or good food. Everything was spent on education and private lessons."

But Stjepan was determined life would be different for his daughters. Following his Uncle Antun's advice, he insisted that the girls concentrate on their studies and learn as many languages as they could because of the opportunities that might afford them in the future.

Not too long before she left Dubrovnik for the U.S., seventeen-year-old Klara was flanked by Mira on the left and Nada on the right.

Klara was in fifth grade when she began taking classes in Russian.

"We had to start studying Russian in school because Yugoslavia was friends with Russia," Klara recalls.

In addition to her schoolwork, Klara was privately tutored in Russian and English by the daughter of a merchant marine captain, whose well-traveled father collected paintings and artifacts from across the world and had them on display in his home.

"I would yell and cry to my father, 'I don't need another lesson!'

but he would tell me, 'Klara, don't forget, the more languages you speak, the more you are worth,'" Klara said.

By the time Klara got to eighth grade, Yugoslavia, while ostensibly Communist, had broken away from the Russian sphere of influence, so the schools dropped their Russian-language requirement.

"That meant I wasted four years learning Russian, but my father was able to find another Russian teacher," Klara said. "I can still read and write Russian because I studied it for eight years. So, after that, I took German in school. I don't know what was behind that, but since we were down on the coast, we had a lot of English and German tourists who came for vacation during the summer. Maybe that was the reason."

Upon his release from prison, Stjepan came home to Dubrovnik and immediately got a job as the director of an export company, which ran the equivalent of a department store.

"They knew how capable he was," Klara said. "He did travel, and he was selling and buying things in Croatia."

But the six months Stjepan spent doing forced labor and his brush with authoritarian rule made him circumspect for the rest of his life. Klara says he never talked about his treatment in prison, even to family members, for fear of potential retaliation. The deprivation he experienced was real: he had been denied his freedom, and that was no way to live.

Stjepan knew the price of freedom in Josip Broz Tito's Yugoslavia. He had been jailed three times for listening to the *Voice of America*, a shortwave radio network emanating from New York with news and commentary designed to counteract Communist propaganda.

"The woman who lived downstairs was snooping and reported him for listening to the radio," Klara said.

Many years later, Stjepan was jailed again on accusations of being a Jewish sympathizer.

Dr. Gerry Cvitanovich, Klara and Drago's younger son, said it is almost incomprehensible to Americans, whose freedom is protected by the Bill of Rights, to imagine such level of governmental and cultural oppression.

"The society they were living in was one in which neighbors were encouraged to spy on each other," Gerry said. "Basically, if they were trying to get a certain person arrested, and someone said something against that person, they would believe the accusation in order to arrest that person."

Such autocratic rule is the reason why—for more than fifty years—Drago's Seafood Restaurant in Metairie has never served a wildly popular brand of vodka to its customers, even though the vodka has no ties to the dictator—Josip Broz Tito—who ran Yugoslavia with an iron fist. Even if it cost them thousands of dollars in sales over the decades, Drago and Klara Cvitanovich would rather lock their doors than serve a drop of "Tito's" Vodka.

Klara and Drago's children and employees love telling that story, which really is a parable explaining an immigrant's passion for freedom.

The sign over the doorpost of King's Landing in the old city of Dubrovnik says it all: "Freedom cannot be sold for all the gold of the world."

3

Nothing Is Beautiful Under Communism

Boxing promoter Don King famously coined the term, "Only in America" to sum up his roller-coaster journey from life as an inmate and street hustler in Cleveland to untold wealth in a seedy, global sport.

King's "Only in America" brand identity always carried with it the echoes of fiction and shameless self-promotion.

Don King never met Drago Cvitanovich, for whom "Only in America" fittingly describes every aspect of a fairy tale life come true.

Where else but in America could a Croatian immigrant—who endured and conquered the twin horrors of WWII and Communist oppression in Yugoslavia, who willed his way to America through unfamiliar testing grounds in Germany and Canada, and who gambled his life's savings to open a small seafood restaurant in Metairie and took out a loan at 20 percent interest to cover the rest of the cost—become, in 1995, for those royal family watchers among us, "Drago, King Argus XI."

Only in America, indeed.

Drago Cvitanovich was the tenth of eleven children born to Dragutin and Bara Cvitanovic' in Igrane, Croatia, about ninety miles northwest of Dubrovnik on the Adriatic coast.

Growing up, he never knew his future wife Klara. How could he? When Drago was seventeen Klara had just been born. They lived far apart in villages near the Adriatic coast.

The second-youngest of the Cvitanovich clan, Drago graduated from the best Franciscan Catholic high school in Croatia—the

Drago's 1954 German passport.

Franciscan Seminary in Sinj (north of the coastal town of Split)—which was a training ground for young men with prospects of becoming Catholic priests. He devoured Latin in the seminary.

"He was destined, probably, to become a priest later on," Klara said. "But the war came, and all that went down the drain."

One of the amazing capacities of the human brain is its ability to store memories despite the onset of dementia. In 2016 and 2017, when Drago was becoming increasingly frail in the months before his death, Klara was astounded by what she heard her husband reciting, almost like a chant.

In their fifty-plus years of marriage, she had never heard him speak to her in this manner.

"He was citing Latin like crazy," Klara said. "He was talking, and I would ask him, 'What are you talking about?' and he would say, 'Oh, I'm thinking of the Latin.'"

For someone who was fluent in Latin, Drago never studied English in school. One of Klara's biggest regrets for Drago was that his English wasn't better. After high school, he attended the University of Zagreb for two years but did not study English. He then went to work, so the opportunity for him to be more facile in English didn't present itself.

"I always felt bad for Drago for his broken English, which, strangely enough, helped him in a lot of cases," Klara said. "He was always funny, and the kids liked it and you could recognize him by it. But, if he had had a better vocabulary—oh, my God, he was a genius. He was brilliant. He would speak sometimes on the level of a philosopher. That was all from high school."

Over the years, Drago's Croatian-spiked English led to some wild encounters that became cherished in family lore, such as the time Klara sent him to a CVS pharmacy to buy Tampax for her—before something got lost in the translation. Unlike most men, Drago loved asking store clerks for directions to save time hunting for an item.

When he came back from the pharmacy, he handed the bag to Klara, who opened the bag before letting out a belly laugh.

"I said I wanted Tampax, not thumb tacks," Klara said.

Drago took the thumb tacks and slammed them on the bar.

That episode of mashed linguistics was one reason local attorney

Albert Nicaud, who waited tables at Drago's for several years to earn money to attend law school, had a button printed, which he always pinned on his waiter's shirt: "Say It In Broken English!"

Drago loved seeing Albert wear the button because he had a self-deprecating sense of humor about being teased.

Drago's eldest sister Mary was the first of the Cvitanovich siblings to forge a new life in America. She left Yugoslavia for the U.S. in 1925 and married, but her first husband, Ante Lulich, died during the Great Depression in 1930.

"As the oldest, she was the bell cow, the matriarch of the family," A. J. Lulich said of his grandmother.

Mary and her husband Ante owned and managed one of Plaquemines Parish's largest orange groves as well as the Lulich Brothers Orange Winery in Buras. After Ante's death, Mary pleaded for help in a letter to her brother, David Cvitanovich. Mary asked him to come to Buras and help out on the farm.

David had left Croatia in 1925, but he went first to New Zealand, where a growing community of 5,000 Croatians was engaged largely in harvesting eucalyptus plants.

"Mary writes to my Dad, 'There's a depression, and I need your help on the orange farm,' and he comes to New Orleans in 1931," recalled David Cvitanovich Jr. Not long after his arrival in Louisiana, David Sr. married Maria Morovich.

Drago's sister Gloria Cvitanovich, born a year before Drago in 1921, landed in the U.S. in 1939 on one of the last ships to leave Yugoslavia before the outbreak of WWII. Gloria wound up in Buras with her elder sister Mary and her brother David. She attended Buras High School for two years to improve her English. In 1947, Gloria was crowned the first queen of the Louisiana Orange Festival and then married Drago Batinich, a native of the Croatian island of Molat.

Gloria and Drago Batinich eventually opened the original Drago's Restaurant at 789 Harrison Avenue in Lakeview in 1952, and they ran it until 1970. To get an idea of the influence of Croatian restaurateurs on New Orleans' food scene, Drago Batinich's brother Sam and his wife Veronica also ran another very successful Uptown seafood restaurant called Sam's Place at 3601 General Taylor Street.

Gloria certainly knew how to run a restaurant.

"Gloria was the wheeler-dealer, a real slicker," David Cvitanovich said of his aunt. "When someone at the Lakeview restaurant asked her for a Bloody Mary, she'd say, 'I won't make you a Bloody *Mary*, but I'll make you a Bloody *Gloria*.'"

Meanwhile, back in Croatia, Drago was doing everything he could to one day escape Communist-controlled Yugoslavia and navigate his way to the United States. Drago never enjoyed talking about his experiences in WWII, when he was conscripted into the Yugoslavian army.

"You could talk to Drago about anything, but never about the war experiences," Klara said. "He was never in an actual fight, but he was on the side of it and he saw it. He would just say, 'Put that aside.' But he did talk about the hunger. They were very, very hungry. When he was stationed in Slovenia (in northwest Croatia), he always talked about how nice it was to get yogurt after so many days of having nothing to eat."

During the war, most of Drago's family, except for himself and his father, fled to Egypt, settling in the region of Mount Sinai, a quasi-biblical, three-year exodus.

"For three years, Drago didn't know anything about his mom," Klara said. "And then, when they came back to Igrane, they came back to nothing in the house. Everything basically had been stolen."

David Cvitanovich Jr. said his mother always told him that the Italian soldiers were more to be feared than the Germans.

"Hitler had made a deal with Mussolini that he was going to give the Italians Dalmatia, and the Italians were very brutal," David said. "They were going to execute our grandfather down at the port. They tied him up and beat him and left him to die. But he was a tough guy, and he survived."

The challenges after the war were monumental, revolving around the lack of food.

"Drago's mother was hiding goats in the house," Klara said. "Drago asked her, 'Why are you taking goats into the house?' And she told him, 'Because I'm not allowed to have any more than three goats, and I have five. Otherwise, the Yugoslav army will confiscate them.' Hunger was the thing that bothered him mostly. And then, after the war, he was very much against Communism. He saw Communist

Drago was a military policeman at a U.S. Army base in Germany in the early 1950s.

rules coming in, and he was basically devastated, because he loved his country. I don't think he ever, in his younger days, dreamed he was going to get out of the country."

Drago's father Dragutin was a fisherman who plied the waters of the Adriatic, sailing south from Igrane along the Adriatic coast to Metković on the Neretva River, bringing fish to sell in Metković and then returning with fresh fruit and vegetables.

Given the amazing success of the Croatian oyster fishing community in South Louisiana, it's a common misconception that Croatians were adept at harvesting oysters before they immigrated to the U.S.

"Absolutely not," Klara said. "They came here, and they didn't know what to do. Oyster fishing was something that someone started in Louisiana, and the Croatians simply developed it."

"The early Croatians were like many Vietnamese are today," said A. J. Lulich, Mary Cvitanovich Lulich's grandson. "They would get a half a dozen of them together, and they would buy one boat, buy two boats, buy three boats, make a pocketful of money and then go back to the old country."

The few oysters harvested in Croatia were in the coastal town of Ston, near Klara's home village of Stupa. Oysters need a mixture of freshwater and saltwater to thrive, and the Croatians perfected a process of cementing small, seed oysters to the branches of a plant resistant to saltwater and then tied them to ropes—which could be pulled up periodically to check on their growth. "But," Klara said, "that labor-intensive process made them very expensive to harvest."

Like his father, Drago was adept as a fisherman, but after WWII, he went to the University of Zagreb and got a job as a census taker. His dream of living in a free land, however, never wavered.

Drago applied for an exit visa, but the Yugoslavian authorities denied his request.

"So, he decided he was going to jump out of Yugoslavia at night time on a little rowboat to get to Italy, but he was caught and put in jail for six months," Klara said. "The guy he was with in the boat was also caught. He went on to become a doctor later in life."

While he was incarcerated, Drago learned of an escape route from other prisoners—going north by car through Slovenia and then into Austria.

"They taught him how to do it by land," Klara recalled. "It was a trip of about 150 miles. He never told me how he did it, but it was secret. It was at night, and he met some people and paid some money. He never gave me their names. By the time he got to Austria, he was in freedom."

For the first time in nearly a decade, Drago was breathing the rarefied air of freedom. The ultimate risk-taker had gambled his life and won. He had overcome authoritarian rule.

"That was tough times, tough times," Drago said in 1995, when, at the age of seventy-two, he was named king of the Krewe of Argus. "It is tough when you have no freedom to think—not just to *say*, but to *think*. Nothing is beautiful under Communism. I never found no place like the United States."

Drago, King Argus XI, loved his adopted country.

Only in America.

On a rainy Mardi Gras in 1995, Drago, surrounded by Tommy and Gerry, reigned as King Argus XI.

4
A Man of Letters

After the devastation of WWII and the steady entrenchment of the Communist regime in Yugoslavia, Stjepan Buconic was more determined than ever that his eldest daughter Klara would someday find her way out of the country to create a new life for herself.

Stjepan was making a decent enough salary in his export business, but he chafed at living under constant surveillance and suspicion.

"Our neighbors spied on my father," Klara said. "He would try to cover up his listening to the radio so nobody could hear."

In school, Klara and her classmates were taught a patriotic song and dance that authorities believed would instill a sense of pride for their homeland among the student body: "We are going! We are working! We are socialism-building!"

"That went on for a few years, and then Socialism turned into Communism, which was devastating," Klara said.

Food continued to be scarce. Klara recalls the life-saving commodities that the U.S. shipped to war-wrecked countries in the late 1940s, spearheaded by President Harry Truman. The *"Trumanova jaja"* (Truman's eggs) weren't exactly tasty—how could powdered eggs taste anything like the real thing?—but they were a major source of protein and eagerly consumed.

"America was sending us cheese, eggs, and milk, and that was the best meal of the day—not just for me, but for a lot of my classmates," Klara said.

In 1951, Klara's passion to one day leave for the United States intensified when the ultra-chic *SS Constitution* docked in Dubrovnik on its maiden voyage. Klara's Aunt Zela, then living in New Jersey across the Hudson River from Manhattan, had a stepson, Nicholas, who was an official photographer on board the *Constitution*. Nicholas invited Klara, then almost thirteen, to tour the luxury vessel for the day.

"It was the first American cruise boat to anchor in Dubrovnik after the war," Klara said of the cruise liner that five years later would escort Grace Kelly across the Atlantic to her fabled wedding with Prince Rainier in Monaco. "When I saw how the people on the boat were dressed, I said to myself, 'Oh my God, I am going to America.' I decided that right then. I knew I was going to America, no matter what."

The *Constitution* story would come full circle many years later.

Klara's brushing elbows with elegance, style, and fashion fueled her commitment to her studies. She excelled at the best high school in Dubrovnik—Gimnazija—and graduated with honors in July 1957.

A letter of support to U.S. officials from her New Jersey-based Aunt Zela earned her an American tourist visa, and, on August 7, 1957, she left Dubrovnik by train for the coastal city of Cherbourg, France, where she transferred to the *Queen Mary* for the trans-Atlantic cruise to New York.

She was eighteen.

While both Klara and her proud father probably knew that her leave-taking would be permanent, Stjepan tried mightily to mask his sorrow. He had wanted this for Klara, after all, since she was a child.

"I was about thirteen when Klara left Dubrovnik, and my father told us he was very happy that she could have a better life and that she could dream and realize the American dream, which she, in fact, did," Klara's youngest sister Mira said. "But later, when Klara was older, our father suffered. When she left for the States, he missed her, and he always said, 'I would give, I don't know what, if Klara was now here with me.' You always have two sides. He wanted her to go and live better, because in those times, people lived very, very hard. I missed her, too. I am very romantic and very sensitive, and very easily I cry."

Drago Cvitanovich, meanwhile, was engaged in a feverish quest of his own to immigrate to the United States. But his plans were much more complicated.

Before he had made his secret escape from Yugoslavia, Drago tried to go through official channels to get to the U.S.

"His sisters (Mary and Gloria) and brother (David) were living in Louisiana and signed papers for him that he would never become a burden on the United States government," Klara said. "And then he waited and waited and nothing happened."

After fleeing Yugoslavia to Austria and then navigating his way to Germany, Drago got a job in the early 1950s as a civilian military police officer for the U.S. Army. He immediately applied for a permanent U.S. visa at the American embassy. However, the U.S. had a fixed quota on the number of permanent visas it would dole out each year to citizens of various European countries, and Drago's application got caught in that numbers crunch.

Once again, Drago waited and waited and nothing happened.

While working on the army base, Drago watched with joy and a touch of envy while his Croatian friends who had applied for visas to Australia, New Zealand, or Canada had much quicker success. Their exit papers were being processed within three to four weeks.

Finally, after three years of getting no response from U.S. immigration officials, Drago reluctantly decided to stop beating his head against a wall. Since he had several relatives and friends in Canada, he applied for a Canadian visa. He received it in two weeks.

Drago was thirty-two in 1954 when he traveled first to Toronto. He had relatives there who hailed from Tucepi, Croatia, just north of his hometown of Igrane. But the cold weather in Toronto and the lack of a steady job prompted him to head west nearly 3,000 miles to Vancouver, British Columbia.

Because of his experience as a fisherman, Drago originally thought he might work the salmon boats near Vancouver Island, but his apprehensive aunt, who lived in Vancouver, would hear nothing of it.

"Absolutely not," she told him. "I will not allow it because I know seven or eight people who have drowned fishing for salmon, and I don't want to lose you."

That's when another friend from Tucepi, who lived in Vancouver, got Drago kitchen work, first in Nanaimo on Vancouver Island and later in the mountains, where he managed the mess hall for a Scottish-owned lumber camp.

"He was the head waiter in the dining room," Klara said. "He was a lousy cook. He was just not a chef."

Still, in 1957, although Drago and Klara were physically located in North America—thousands of miles apart, Drago in British Columbia and Klara in New Jersey—the two Croatians knew nothing of each other.

That was about to change. A funny thing happened as Klara took the train to Cherbourg, France, to catch the *Queen Mary* to the U.S. Her itinerary from Dubrovnik called for her to make a layover of several days in Zagreb, the capital of Croatia. In Zagreb, she stayed with Nada Hocevar, a friend of the family and a former school inspector who used to stay at the Buconic house when she was in Dubrovnik on a school assignment.

"Our family's home in Dubrovnik was like an Airbnb," Klara recalled, "and every time Nada came to Dubrovnik, she stayed with us, and we became very close. So, when I went to Zagreb and she found out I was going to America, she said, 'Oh my God, I'm going to let *Drago* know that a Croatian girl is coming to America!'"

As it turned out, years earlier, when Drago was studying at the University of Zagreb after the war and then worked for the census office, he had rented a room in Nada Hocevar's mother's house.

Nada showed Klara a picture of Drago that her mom had taken.

"I said, 'He's cute.' That's all I said," Klara recalled, laughing. "And then I forgot about it."

But when Aunt Zela greeted Klara upon her arrival at New York harbor, her first question came out of left field. She had in her hands several letters that Drago had written to Klara after he had gotten her forwarding address in the U.S. from Nada Hocevar, the school inspector in Croatia.

"Who's the jackass who's writing you a letter every day?" Aunt Zela asked Klara.

Klara smiled sheepishly and told her the story about the "mysterious Drago," whose only contact until that point was a black-and-white picture she was shown during her temporary stay in Zagreb before she departed for the U.S.

Then Klara took the handful of letters and started reading.

"Basically, in the letters, he gave me a history of himself," Klara said. "I just put them aside and didn't worry about it."

Displaying a trait that would become his hallmark, Drago was

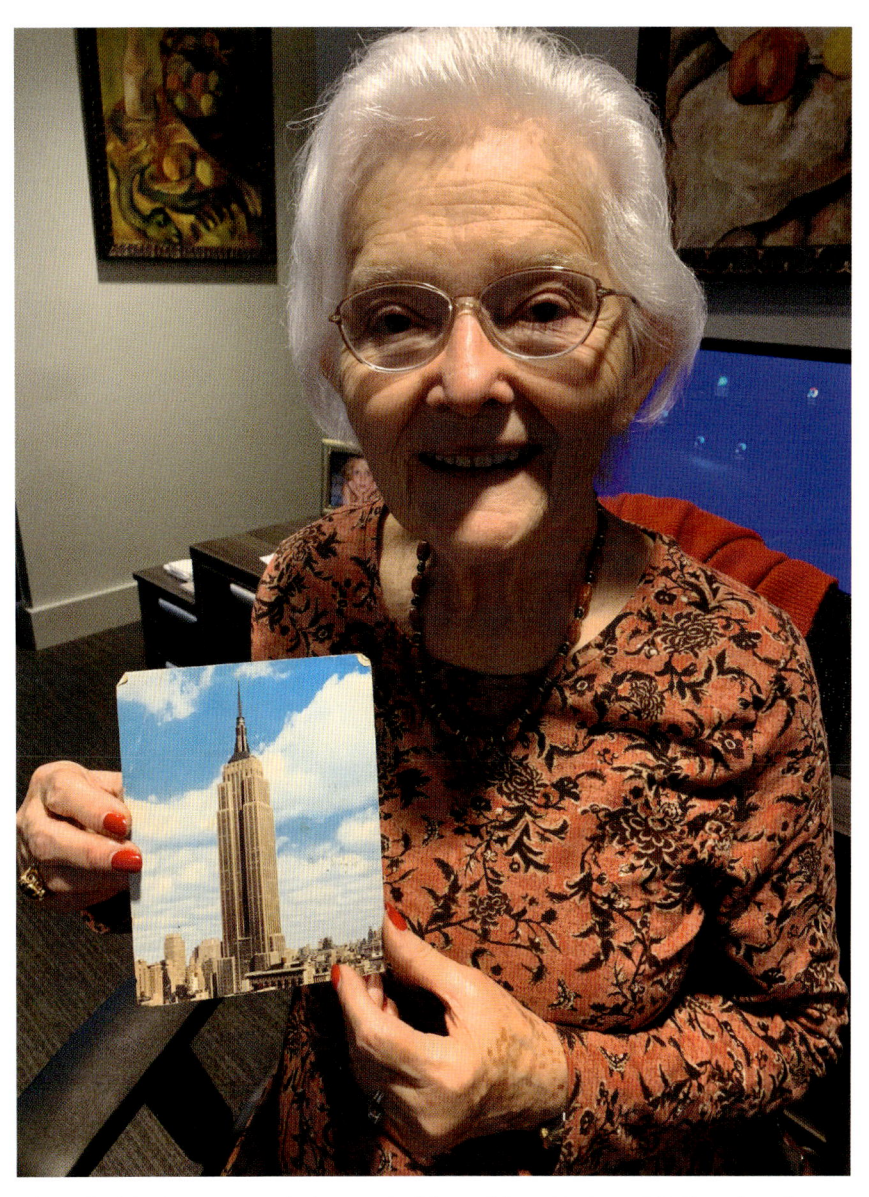

Klara holds the postcard she mailed from New York in 1958 to her former high school classmates in Croatia after arriving in the U.S. on the Queen Mary.

persistent, continuing to write. In early 1958, Drago let Klara know that he was planning a trip to New Orleans for Mardi Gras to visit his two sisters and his brother. He had the time because the lumber yard was on strike.

Klara also had family in the New Orleans area. Her father's two first cousins—Jelka and Violet—had landed in New Orleans in the 1930s. Violet Morovich's daughter was married to a Columbia University student, and they also were planning to go to New Orleans for Mardi Gras in February 1958 to visit family.

"Why don't you come down with us for Mardi Gras?" her cousin Violet asked, assuring Klara they could stay with her relatives in New Orleans. "We're going to be down there for two weeks."

Klara did not think that Drago's letter about his planned trip to Mardi Gras and her cousin's invitation to attend Mardi Gras were coincidental.

"When his letter came, I thought to myself, 'This is something that's made in heaven by God, because this could not happen in any other way," she said. "So, I told Violet, 'I'm going with you to New Orleans for Mardi Gras.'"

As Klara readied herself to leave New Jersey in February 1958 for what she expected would be a fun two weeks in New Orleans, Aunt Zela's husband hugged her at the door of his fifth-floor apartment, which overlooked the Hudson River and the Empire State Building, and offered a confounding farewell.

"I don't know how my aunt's husband got this feeling in his head, but when my cousin came to pick me up to leave for the flight to New Orleans, he opened the door of the apartment for me and said, 'Goodbye Mala Klara (Little Klara), I'll never see you again,'" Klara said. "I said, 'Oh yes you will, in two weeks, blah, blah, blah.' And the rest is history."

On Saturday, March 22, 1958—forty days after meeting a handsome, fellow immigrant from Croatia, thirty-two days after Mardi Gras and twenty-one days after her nineteenth birthday—Klara Buconic walked down the aisle of Our Lady of Good Harbor Catholic Church in Buras and married Drago Cvitanovich.

5
Mardi Gras Romance

"I knew after the first two days that, yes, I'm going to marry Drago."

There have been whirlwind romances, but not many have spun more deliciously out of control than the one that swirled around Klara and Drago in February 1958.

She had seen a picture of Drago before, of course, but as he walked across the tarmac of Moisant Field and sauntered through the terminal door, Klara was swept away by just about everything she was witnessing in real life: his strength, his ready smile, and his good humor.

"He was darned good looking, he had a great personality, and he was a great writer," Klara recalled.

Drago's sister Mary and brother David lived in Buras, and his sister Gloria lived in New Orleans. Drago and Klara were in New Orleans nearly every night to catch a parade.

For the first time in her life, Klara ate cotton candy.

The swirl was real.

"It was just fun—I couldn't believe myself," Klara recalled. "I was, should I say,

The man with a smile a mile wide—which lasted a lifetime—captured Klara's heart.

in heaven. I thought I was. It was totally different from anything I had ever experienced."

Did she see Rex on Canal Street?

"We went to see everything," Klara said. "I really didn't understand what was going on. Drago asked me what I wanted to eat. I said, 'Hot dogs. I love hot dogs.'"

At some point after Mardi Gras (Fat Tuesday was February 18 that year), Drago, then thirty-five, felt he had no more time to waste. Klara would turn nineteen on March 1.

"He just said, 'Are you ready to marry me?'" Klara said, laughing. "Plain, old, 'Are you ready to marry me?' And I said, 'Yes!'"

Those formalities concluded, the couple drove to Schwegmann's supermarket on Old Gentilly Road in New Orleans, at that time the largest grocery store in the world at 155,000 square feet. Schwegmann's was Walmart before Walmart, where customers could buy groceries, beer, liquor, prescription drugs, clothes, car tires, and batteries and also get their hair cut or see a dentist.

Schwegmann's also sold jewelry.

"We bought the ring at Schwegmann's," Klara said. "It cost either $259 or $359."

On her left ring finger, to this day, is the ring Drago bought her at Schwegmann's.

"It was a wedding ring and engagement ring together," Klara said. "He also updated it later with another ring with a larger stone for our fortieth anniversary, but I have worn the ring he gave me to this day. I have never taken it off."

While Klara had no misgivings about agreeing to marry a man she had known for barely a month, others in her family sounded the alarm. Her Aunt Zela in New Jersey was upset with the massive rush—"she thought I might be staying with her for the rest of my life"—and her father Stjepan was concerned, not exactly because of the quick engagement, but about the age difference between his daughter and Drago.

"He trusted me on knowing Drago, but he said, 'I just want you to remember, you are going to be forty, and Drago is going to be fifty-seven or whatever. Drago's too old for you.' I just went back on him and said, 'Well, you are ten years older than Mom!'"

Stjepan Buconic, Klara's father (middle), was a highly successful entrepreneur in Croatia whose hard-earned property and personal belongings were seized after WWII by General Tito's Communist regime.

    Klara's mother Marija had the same concerns about the age difference.

    "Just think about how old you will be when he is ninety—do you have any problem about that?" Marija asked her daughter.

    "No."

    "Okay, then."

    "They were also worried that I did not know Drago long enough," Klara recalled. "They didn't know anything about him, about his past or his future. It was just, I guess, not knowing. Everybody tried to stop it. But, I'm going to tell you, it worked. Everybody loved Drago once they knew him. It was just that nobody knew Drago."

    For centuries, the Croatian marriage tradition had been for the prospective groom to be significantly older than his prospective bride.

    "There was a saying that a man couldn't get married until he planted thirty olive trees—because you had to produce to support a wife," Klara said. "That was for the people who were farmers, but even outside the farms, that saying still held true."

Klara said she never thought for a second that she was rushing into anything.

"It never, ever, ever entered my mind," she said. "Mind you, I was treated like a queen. Anything I wanted, I had. There was never an argument. You know, some people throw pots and pans—never! None of that. It was always, 'Okay, baby; whatever you want, baby.'"

Klara and Drago's wedding reception was held in the packing shed of the Lulich Brothers Orange Winery in Buras, which stayed in business until repeated freezes and hurricanes in the early 1960s shut down both the orange harvest and the winery.

"That orange wine was delicious—it was eighteen to twenty proof," said A. J. Lulich, Drago's nephew.

After leaving New Orleans, the newlyweds honeymooned for two

Klara and Drago cut their wedding cake after exchanging vows at Our Lady of Good Harbor Catholic Church in Buras. Klara was nineteen and Drago was thirty-five.

Klara and Drago were married on Saturday, March 22, 1958—forty days after meeting each other in New Orleans for Mardi Gras. They were married for fifty-nine years.

weeks in San Francisco, staying for two days in a hotel and then accepting the gift of a free room from a widower from Igrane who knew Drago's family.

"We thought, why not? We didn't want to spend all our money," Klara said.

They finally made their way north to Seattle, about 140 miles south of the British Columbia border. While Drago's Canadian visa allowed him to cross the border to resume his work at the lumber mill's mess hall, Klara needed to wait three months for her Canadian visa to come through. When it did, she traveled north to embark on another adventure of love and shared sacrifice.

The honeymooners' first home, in the middle of a Canadian forest, was a twenty-eight-by-eight-foot trailer.

6
Special Delivery

The Douglas firs and lodgepole pines of the Lillooet Ranges near Seton Portage in British Columbia are breathtaking, but for a nineteen-year-old newlywed from the other side of the world, the vibrant natural canvas and pristine air could capture her attention for only so long.

"The mountains were beautiful, but there was nothing to do," Klara Cvitanovich said, recalling her first impressions of the new frontier she encountered as a young Croatian-Canadian wife.

Tommy Cvitanovich, the elder of Klara and Drago's two sons, remembers his dad telling him a story of how Drago got chased up a tree by a bear.

"He didn't realize until then that a bear could climb a tree," Tommy said, laughing.

The trees were beautiful, but Klara felt stirred to do more. Drawing on her educational background and her passion for learning, Klara took correspondence courses with the University of British Columbia. Her professors there soon became intrigued by her background.

"They asked me if I would teach English as a Second Language (ESL) courses for them because they had so many Croatian immigrants who spoke no English at all," Klara said. "This was a time when so many people of Croatia were running out of Yugoslavia."

Klara wound up teaching ESL classes to Croatian immigrants who lived near her trailer camp.

"I didn't want to go to another village to teach, and Drago didn't want me to do that, either," she said.

Tommy was born in Vancouver on May 3, 1959, a family addition that began to make their narrow trailer feel as wide as a sardine can. Eighteen months later, on Nov. 10, 1960, their second son, Gerry, was born, making things feel even more claustrophobic.

"When I was pregnant with Gerry, Tommy would yell out, 'Momma, move!' because he couldn't pass me by," Klara said. "So, we bought a bigger trailer—forty-eight feet long—and in this one we felt like we were in heaven. The boys had their rooms, and it was nice and roomy."

Then, out of nowhere, Drago's and Klara's lives changed with another special delivery—this one from Western Union in 1961.

Deep in the Canadian woods, Klara and Drago learned through a telegram that the American visa application Drago had submitted about ten years earlier in Belgrade finally had come through.

"After all that time we had given up hope," Klara said. "It hit us like thunder in a clear sky. The telegram said our entry to the U.S. had been approved, and we had eight days to enter the country."

In the early 1960s—in the family tiny trailer in the British Columbia forest—Drago opened a bottle of orange wine distilled at the Lulich Brothers Orange Winery in Buras, Louisiana.

Eight. Not eighty.

"We had to get rid of everything we had," Klara said. "We had just bought the forty-eight-foot trailer four or five months earlier and a brand-new car. We gave the car back. We sold what we could, but it was not much. We put all that together, and it was $2,300. We took a loss on the trailer, but it didn't matter. We bought train tickets from Vancouver to Spokane, Washington to Chicago and then to New Orleans. And, I tell you what, both kids got sick on the trip from the motion. It was miserable."

Klara and Drago didn't have the foggiest idea where they would stay once they arrived in New Orleans with their two sons and three suitcases on June 12, 1961—the eve of the Catholic Feast of St. Anthony of Padua—"but we knew we could work it out with the whole family."

They stayed first with Klara's Morovich cousins and then got an apartment in New Orleans' Lakeview neighborhood, where Drago's sister Gloria and her husband Drago Batinich had been running their successful Drago's Restaurant on Harrison Avenue since 1952.

Their first apartment was located about ten blocks from the restaurant, making it easy for Drago to walk to work.

"We didn't have a car, and he didn't want to have to depend on anybody picking him up," Klara said. "He enjoyed walking, and he walked to work every day. Sometimes people would see him walking and offer him a ride."

Eventually, Drago bought a used car from a fellow Croatian—a Franciscan priest named Father Joseph Simic—who was returning to the home country.

Drago made an instant impact at his sister's restaurant. The bar was located directly to the left inside the front-door entrance at 789 Harrison Avenue, and Drago served beer and mixed drinks and shucked oysters, using his broken English and hearty laugh to build rapport with the regulars. That restaurant later became the long-time location for Landry's and is now known as Junior's.

"Drago was bartender, oyster shucker, garbageman—whatever was needed in the restaurant, he did it," Klara said. "He had to learn how to shuck oysters because he had never done it before. He took care of the place like it was his own. He was beloved."

With four-month-old Gerry on her lap and Tommy looking on, Klara had her hands full in the Canadian woods in March 1961, just several months before she and Drago received U.S. visas.

The regulars and the employees were so enamored of Drago's easygoing personality that they gave him the nickname "Brother-in-Law." The two dining rooms in Drago's usually were packed on Friday and Saturday nights, attracting repeat business because of the consistency of the food and the service.

"You could walk into the place any night and see the same people," Klara said. "It was where Lakeview people went for beer and oysters."

Drago took home seventy-five dollars a week, and Gloria gave him a ten to twenty dollar tip on Friday nights. In addition, Gloria asked Klara, who was not involved with the restaurant, to iron clothes for her for seven dollars a day while she was caring for her two young sons at home. But that proposition ended when Klara's mother, Marija, and Klara's Aunt Zela visited her in New Orleans.

"My mom was very upset and she told me, 'You didn't go to

When Klara's mother Marija came to visit her daughter in New Orleans in August 1963, they took a picture with Tommy and Gerry atop the Orleans Avenue Canal in Lakeview, across the street from their home.

school to do this. If you can't work this out, I want you to come home,'" Klara said.

Klara agreed. She decided to scour the classifieds for a job. One ad in particular fascinated her: the American Automobile Association (AAA) was looking for a travel agent.

"I decided I would love to have a job with a travel agency because then I could get a discount to travel to Croatia," she said. "Sometimes travel agents could get 75 percent off on travel, and I hadn't been back to Croatia in many years. I wanted to see my mom and dad and my sisters."

The next day, she went to the AAA office and interviewed for the job with the lead travel agent, Flo Cleveland.

"I didn't have any experience, but Flo was very nice, God bless her soul," Klara said. "I had done a little tour guide work for a couple of summers in Dubrovnik. Flo was ready to hire me right then and there, but she said she had to talk to her boss and would let me know the next day."

The phone call from Flo came the next day.

"Honey, my boss says you don't type, so you don't qualify for the job," Flo told her.

"Wait a second," Klara replied. "I don't need typing for the job."

"Well, I'm sorry, that's what the boss says," Flo said.

Rather than wallow in her disappointment, Klara returned to the classifieds, searching for a place that would teach her how to type. She circled Meadows-Draughon Business College, a secretarial school on Canal Street across from Warren Easton High School that also taught bookkeeping and accounting.

"I wanted to type forty words a minute, and I wanted to take accounting," Klara said. "I typed from 9:00 a.m. to 3:00 p.m. for two weeks. I was determined I was going to type. After two weeks, I got a certificate that I was typing forty words a minute. I also needed a break from all that typing, so I took an accounting course. God gave me the brains."

Armed with her new skills, Klara went back to the classifieds: AAA was still advertising for a travel agent. She went back to the office on Marigny Street in Gentilly.

"Flo looked at me and said, 'Honey, it's the same job you just applied for,' and I said, 'Yes, but I can type. Here's my certificate,'" Klara said. "She looked kind of stunned and said she would let me know the next day. I found out later she went to her boss, Mr. Foley, and said, 'If you don't hire her, here's my resignation.' He asked her if she felt that strongly about me, and she said, 'Yes, I do.' So, he said, 'Hire her.' God bless Flo Cleveland."

Klara found out a year later that the real reason her boss hesitated in hiring her was because of her Croatian accent. He was married to a woman from the Netherlands.

"He didn't want to hear her voice at home and my voice at the office!" Klara said, laughing.

Klara did not drive then, so Drago brought her to work at the AAA office near current-day Brother Martin High School and picked her up every evening before he went back to work at the restaurant.

Klara was able to work outside the home only because she and Drago arranged for full-time help to watch their two young sons. Klara asked her younger cousin Vera—their grandfathers were brothers—to come from Croatia to the United States to serve as kind of an "older sister" to Tommy and Gerry.

Vera was just seventeen at the time, but she attended Delgado Community College during the day—Drago drove her there and picked her up—and then was at home when the boys came home from school.

"I was just graduating from high school, and they asked me if I wanted to come to New Orleans," Vera recalled. "I was young, so I said, 'Why not?' We didn't have anything in Croatia, so it was a good opportunity to come here. Most of my English language came from Tommy and Gerry because I stayed with them. I spoke Croatian to them, and they spoke English to me. After school, we would go over those children's books that had things like: 'See Spot run!' It was an honor for me that I was able to do it. The boys were good. They listened to me. Tommy always said he listened to me like I was his big sister."

"I needed someone I could trust with the kids," Klara said. "Drago would bring Vera to Delgado every morning at eight so that she could study advertising and art, and then he would pick her up at three. She went home to watch the boys, and Drago went to work from three to midnight. The boys were never on the street after school. Somebody was always home. I believed in total control so they would not run wild."

Bow ties and seersucker suits for Tommy and Gerry in the 1960s.

At work, Klara strengthened AAA's international travel bookings by attending a professional development workshop in Little Rock, Arkansas, and learning the nuances of the trade.

Word was beginning to spread about the dynamo from Croatia who was selling a lot of vacations. One day, Klara got a call from W. H. Worden, head of the D. H. Holmes travel agency on Canal Street, who asked her how much money she was making a week.

"$325," Klara told him.

"You can start Monday at $350," Worden replied.

"I can't do that because I have to give two weeks' notice," Klara said. "He was mad, but that was the right thing to do."

Drago and Klara treated Klara's younger cousin Vera like their own daughter, handling all the details for her 1967 wedding at St. Dominic Church. Vera was nineteen when she married insurance agent Anthony Occhipinti.

After giving her notice to AAA, Klara transferred to D. H. Holmes on Canal Street. Drago would bring her to work at nine thirty in the morning, and she would stay until five thirty in the afternoon and catch the number eighty express bus to Lakeview and walk four blocks to their home on Orleans Avenue, right behind Hynes Elementary School.

"I had my umbrella, boots, and a raincoat in case it rained," Klara said. "It was a hard life, but that job guaranteed that my boys were going to have the best schools and that I had a payment for my house. It assured us that we were going to succeed."

Two or three times a year, Klara led major tours of Europe that she booked through Caravan Tours, which required her to be away from home for at least two weeks. She always managed to use those trips to reconnect with her family in Yugoslavia.

"It was very well planned so that when we got to Rome, I would block out a day and a half for me to fly to Dubrovnik to visit my family and then fly back to meet the tour in Monte Carlo," Klara said. "We had a really good tour guide who took care of things when I was visiting my family. It worked out perfectly."

In short order, Klara exponentially expanded the international travel business at D. H. Holmes. She not only knew the ins and outs of international travel, but she also had been versed since childhood in European history and geography. That combination was hard for any local agent to beat.

Her full skill set was put to the test one day when a wealthy woman from New Orleans came into D. H. Holmes with a composition book and a special request: she was ready to embark on "the trip of a lifetime"—forty-five days around Europe. The woman had circled London, Paris, and Rome and many other must-see destinations. As she handed Klara the composition book filled with her specific instructions, she told her she was bidding out the proposal to two other local travel agents.

"It was like a travel agency exam," Klara said. "She wanted the entire tour to be escorted, and she didn't want to lose time anywhere."

Klara brought the book home at night and went to work. Within a week, she called the woman back.

"I have it ready for you. You can pick it up whenever you want," Klara told her.

The woman was so stunned by the quick response that "she almost didn't believe me," Klara said.

The other travel agents were still working on their proposals. A day late and a dollar short. Klara got the business.

"I felt like I was on top of New York," she said.

Klara increased the travel business at D. H. Holmes so significantly that Billy Worden, director William Worden's son, came to her one day and told her: "Start making out your check for $450."

By that time, Klara had four people working for her, including a secretary.

She didn't have to type anymore.

7
Gut Check

It's funny how childhood memories stick.

In September 1965, Tommy Cvitanovich was six and a half and Gerry was nearly five, but they can remember in vivid detail where they were and what happened as Hurricane Betsy approached New Orleans.

The family's Orleans Avenue house, one block from Hynes Elementary School, was directly on the west wall of the Orleans Avenue Canal. Klara and Drago decided it would be safer for the family to hunker down at the restaurant, ten blocks away. The building at 789 Harrison Avenue had a second story.

"I don't have a very good long-term memory," Gerry said, "but I do remember riding out Hurricane Betsy at Drago's and then going outside when the eye passed over."

Drago's Restaurant served as a shelter of last resort for multiple branches of the Cvitanovich family. Gloria Cvitanovich Batinich and her husband Drago Batinich, who owned Drago's, initially offered their home on Emerald Street in Lakeshore—right behind the Robert E. Lee Theater and close to Lake Pontchartrain—to Gloria's brother David's family, who lived in Buras, sixty miles south of New Orleans.

But when New Orleans police rolled down their Lakeshore street with bullhorns calling for a mandatory evacuation of all residents north of Robert E. Lee (now Allen Toussaint) Boulevard, they, too, hauled off to the restaurant to ride out Betsy.

David Cvitanovich Jr., who had just turned ten, recalls his cousins and sister Barbara "lying in the booths on the Memphis Street side of the restaurant. A doggone tornado hit the Winn-Dixie across the street and smashed all the windows. I'll never forget having to get the pots to catch the water where it was leaking through."

The restaurant recovered quickly with the brilliant kitchen work of a pair of African American cooks, "Mama Ruth" Jenkins and Anna Thomas, and the hard-working team led by Drago and Gloria Batinich, Drago "Brother-in-Law" Cvitanovich and other staffers such as Mildred, Clarence, and Legendre.

Klara and Drago felt they finally were establishing a firm foothold in New Orleans. They had two decent salaries, their kids were happy in school—Tommy pitched in by bussing a few tables and cleaning some dishes on Friday and Saturday nights—and they were saving for the day they might be able to open a restaurant of their own. Based on conversations Drago had with his sister Gloria and her husband, Drago Batinich, Klara and Drago were certain that the Lakeview restaurant would be offered to them after the Batiniches had finished putting their two daughters, Mary Ann and Joan, through college.

Under Drago's watchful eye, Gerry learned early how to find the sweet spot in shucking oysters. He has a few scars to prove it.

Klara always kept her eye on the cash flow and made sure the family had enough to pay its bills.

Several months before Hurricane Betsy in 1965, Chris Matulich, a fellow Croatian who owned Chris Steak House on Broad Street in New Orleans, approached Drago and asked if he might be interested in buying his restaurant. Klara recalled Matulich telling Drago he wouldn't even have to put up any money on the front end to buy the steak house.

"Chris said, 'I will teach you and your wife everything you need to know to run the restaurant. You'll be able to pay for the restaurant in less than a year,'" Klara said.

The deal might have amounted to about $30,000.

While Drago was grateful for the enticing offer, he passed because he felt his long-term future was tied to taking over his sister Gloria's restaurant someday, when her daughters were settled and married.

Matulich eventually sold Chris Steak House in May 1965 for $22,000 to Ruth Fertel, a single mother with no business experience who went on to become one of the most successful restaurateurs of all time. Fertel planted the Ruth's Chris Steak House flag across North America and was a pioneer in upscale franchising.

"Ruth made that place terrific," Klara said. "I was so happy for her."

But, sometimes, life gets in the way of dreams. Gloria and Drago Batinich decided not to sell their restaurant to Drago and Klara. Family is family and business is business, but this one cut deeply.

How Klara found out that the Lakeview restaurant would not be sold to them is something that, with the benefit of twenty-twenty hindsight, lit a motivational fire that fueled the creation of a restaurant empire surpassing Drago's and Klara's wildest imagination.

Klara was at home with Tommy and Gerry one day when a family friend, Ben Bilich, a fellow Croatian, knocked on her door. Klara was understandably preoccupied because a few days earlier, Gerry had taken a baseball to the face, and she was making preparations for his surgery the next day to repair a broken nose.

Ben was carrying a plate of figs.

"The plate of figs was an excuse for him to leave the house to visit us," Klara said. "He said, 'Klara, I'm sorry for what I am coming here for, but it's not to deliver figs. I have some news for you.'"

Ben had grown close to Klara and Drago because every Monday

night, Tommy and Gerry would go to the Bilich house to play with their children.

"Tommy and Gerry loved going over there and playing with their toys," Klara said.

But Ben was even closer friends with Gloria and Drago Batinich. Ben was born in the same village as Drago Batinich; hence, the inner tension Ben felt as he delivered the figs.

Ben told Klara he had heard that Drago Batinich had closed a deal to sell his restaurant—but not to Drago and Klara. The process of the sale, Ben told Klara, was that Drago and the other employees would be informed sometime in the near future and would be given one month's notice before the restaurant switched hands.

"I didn't want you to have one month's notice," Ben told Klara. "I want to give you three months' notice. But, please, don't tell anybody. My wife doesn't know anything about my visit here."

Klara absorbed the words in stunned disbelief.

"When we found out that they sold the place to someone else, Drago was crushed," Klara said. "He was crying like a baby, I'll never forget that. I begged him to leave immediately, but he said, 'No, I'm going to stay and see this through.' He didn't want to give notice until after his sister and brother-in-law told him to his face that they were selling to someone else."

No one knows exactly what prompted Gloria and Drago Batinich's decision to sell to someone outside the family. Perhaps Gloria and her husband did not want to take on an owner-financed sale, where they would have to be paid over several years and not up front. Perhaps they were unsure about Drago's and Klara's ability to maintain the restaurant's level of success.

"Their excuse was that we didn't have any money and I was not a 'restaurant girl'—I was an 'office girl,'" Klara said. "So, I was going to prove to her and everybody else that I could do both."

The bottom line is the decision cut deeply, but it also fueled a passion.

A few weeks later after officially getting word of the sale, Drago packed up his oyster knife and moved to Acme Oyster House in the French Quarter. In time, with Drago's ability to transform pain into motivation, the world once again would be his oyster.

In later years, the family tensions, while never forgotten, soothed.

Gloria's two daughters, Mary Ann and Joan, both tragically preceded their mother in death. As Mary Ann Batinich Mikasinovich, a former class president at Loyola University New Orleans, became very sick, Klara made sure Drago's delivered her favorite food to her home every night.

When Gerry was suffering from a mysterious illness as a teenager, Gloria ran into Klara at D. H. Holmes in Lakeside Shopping Center one day and called out to her from behind.

"I'm sorry to hear the news about Gerry," Gloria told Klara. "My family and I want to donate blood for him if need be."

In time, Klara, Drago, Tommy, and Gerry wound up spending holidays with the Batinich family, and Gloria Batinich frequently ate at Drago's in Metairie. Drago and Klara also hosted an anniversary party for Drago and Gloria at the original Drago's restaurant on Harrison Avenue, which was now known as Landry's.

Drago, seated second from left, and his brother-in-law Drago Batinich, third from left.

In 1976, a few years after opening his own restaurant in Metairie, Drago shucked oysters for his growing clientele. His sister Gloria had already sold her Lakeview restaurant, the original Drago's.

Even Tommy and Gerry experienced the reconciliation with the Batinich family.

"When my first child was born, we went to visit Teta [Aunt] Gloria's house before we took her home to our own house," Gerry recalled.

At Gloria Batinich's Funeral Mass in 2006—celebrated at St. Dominic Church in Lakeview—Tommy, Gerry, Dave Cvitanovich, and A. J. Lulich served as pallbearers. They rode in a limousine behind the hearse as it made a U-turn on Harrison Avenue and passed in front of the original Drago's Restaurant, which then was still closed after Katrina.

"As we passed the restaurant, I kid you not, the freaking front door just swung wide open with the wind as the hearse in front of us was passing by," Gerry recalled. "It was the spookiest thing. I remember everybody getting goosebumps. The door didn't just open a little. That sucker swung wide open and stayed open, because I yelled out and all the other pallbearers saw it. All the other guys in the limo saw it too. It was as though Gloria was at the door of the restaurant saying, 'Good to see you, baby!'"

Even Drago, who carried with him the sting of family rejection, softened with the passage of time. In 1995 at the Krewe of Argus ball, Drago was up on stage, greeting members of his royal court and posing for pictures with krewe members.

That was fine, but all Drago was interested in right then and there was gathering the entire Cvitanovich clan for a wide-angle family picture. The captains of Argus were shouting out to Drago and trying to get his attention because they wanted to introduce him to actor Steven Seagal, who was the grand marshal that year.

"If you can remember back then, Steven Seagal was a pretty big deal," Gerry said, laughing. "Drago didn't have a clue who he was. He said, 'I don't give a damn who Steven Seagal is. I'm looking for my sister Gloria.'"

Seagal heard the exchange and had a belly laugh.

After all, family is family.

8
"We Did a Good Thing"

If there was anything positive about Drago's involuntary move to Acme Oyster House on Iberville Street in the French Quarter, it was that his new place of employment was located only two blocks from D. H. Holmes at 921 Canal Street, where Klara was working as a lead travel agent. That meant it was a lot easier for Drago and Klara to coordinate their daily commuting schedules.

Drago could take Klara to work and then be available to start shucking oysters right away. The close proximity of their parents' workplaces also allowed Tommy and Gerry, then ages ten and eight, to take the public service bus—NOPSI's number eighty express—from Lakeview into the Central Business District after school, mostly to visit their mom.

"I must have been eight or nine years old, and I was taking guitar lessons at Werlein's on Canal Street," Gerry said, laughing. "Tommy got stuck with accordion lessons. We would visit my dad sometimes. The oyster bar was to the right when you walked into Acme, and my dad would be there shucking oysters."

The odd thing is, Gerry never developed a taste for oysters on the half shell.

"I didn't like oysters, and I didn't like fish," Gerry said. "To this day, I still cannot eat certain types of fish. I still don't like oysters unless they're charbroiled. But I can eat charbroiled all day!"

After Drago's departure from the Harrison Avenue restaurant, Klara and Drago focused on saving every penny so they could open their own place one day.

Drago felt the critical factor in the success of any new restaurant venture—beyond possessing the financial wherewithal to withstand the significant start-up costs—was assembling a superb, back-of-the-house kitchen staff. He intuitively understood that "Mama Ruth" Jenkins and Anna Thomas, the kitchen duo at the original Drago's on Harrison, and as many of the kitchen staff as he could round up (Mildred, Solomon, Jessie, and Legendre), had to be a part of any new restaurant he wanted to open.

"He knew Mama Ruth and Anna Thomas were coming, and that was important," Tommy said. "Probably, even to this day, nobody has ever cooked more food for me than Mama Ruth, and she's been gone for more than twenty years. She made unbelievable gumbo and red gravy. That's where I learned to put sugar in red gravy. If there was one dish that I knew I couldn't get any more and you'd give me one pass to get the recipe back, it would be her crawfish bisque. She took that dish to her grave."

As Klara and Drago began to assemble a plan for their new restaurant, the most obvious question was its location. Drago had attracted a loyal following in Lakeview, but the population of Jefferson Parish was booming in the late 1960s and early 1970s.

The original two-lane span of the Causeway bridge over Lake Pontchartrain opened in 1956, and Lakeside Shopping Center in Metairie opened in 1960, attracting customers away from Canal Street in part because of the ease of parking. The northbound span of the Causeway opened in 1969, fueling another stage of growth in Jefferson and St. Tammany parishes. Shell roads in Metairie were being paved over with asphalt daily.

Real estate agent Bob Loupe, a former regular at the Drago's Restaurant on Harrison, kept in touch with Drago after he left Lakeview.

"Jefferson Parish is where everything is coming," Loupe kept telling Drago. "This is where you're going to make a killing."

The parcel of wilderness land at 3232 North Arnoult Road in Metairie—where Drago's restaurant stands today—cost $19,000. At the time they purchased the lot, Klara said, "There was nothing between us and the lake. It was bush. It was so backwoods."

Klara and Drago looked at four or five places before buying the lot from the family of Genevieve B. Gordon, which owned two adjacent parcels in what Jefferson Parish called the "Hessmer Farms" tract.

"The lot cost $19,000, and it cost another $100,000 to build and equip the restaurant," Klara said. "So, we were like $120,000 all in. We put in everything we had."

But their savings didn't cover all that was needed to open the doors. They took out a loan arranged by a good friend, Conrad Meyer III, a director with Pelican Homestead, who had dined regularly at the Drago's on Harrison.

"Conrad loved Drago," Klara said. "He had three sons, and they would come in every Friday night and ask, 'Uncle Drago, how are your oysters today?' and he would give each boy an oyster."

They also borrowed a large chunk of money at 20 percent interest from Safety Finance, a savings and loan in which Croatian fishermen had invested their money over many decades. The going interest rate on regular commercial loans at that time was about 8.5 percent, but Drago and Klara hadn't come this far to blink at a 20 percent loan.

"The fact that Drago borrowed the money at a very high interest rate—and to go to a laundromat with the kids late at night to wash the tablecloths—tells you everything you need to know," said Eddie Esposito, a high school and college friend of Tommy's and a former Drago's waiter who went on to become a business consultant, largely in the restaurant field. "They are the classic immigrant-American entrepreneurial story. You've got to believe in what you're doing, you've got to be passionate about what you're doing, and you can't be waffling around all the time."

Still, as the clock ticked toward possible opening day, Drago remained a little short of all the funds he needed.

Once again, the extended Cvitanovich family provided a safety net. Mary Cvitanovich Mahoney and her brother Andrew Cvitanovich— who opened Mary Mahoney's Old French House restaurant in Biloxi, Mississippi, in 1964—and Drago were first cousins. (Mary and Andrew's father, Anthony, and Drago's mother, Bara, were brother and sister.) The extended Cvitanovich clan got together regularly for Sunday dinners in Biloxi, and the Easter Sunday gathering was a can't-miss affair, with the outgoing Mary serving as party planner and as the catalyst of *joie de vivre*.

Klara said somehow, Mary found out, probably through her uncle Tom Cvitanovich, that the New Orleans Cvitanoviches were a little short on the cash they needed to open their new venture.

Mary had known from personal experience about how challenging it was to get a restaurant off the ground. After her lounge had been forced out of the Tivoli Hotel in Biloxi in the early 1960s, it took her, her husband Bob Mahoney, and her brother Andrew Cvitanovich two years to turn a $13,000 loan and the sale of Andrew's shrimp boat into the renovation of the oldest building in Biloxi for their new restaurant.

Drago and Klara were now in a similar predicament. They were on the cusp of launching their own American dream, but they were tapped out.

"We didn't have all the money we needed to buy the food, and the silverware, and the tablecloths," Klara recalled. "So, Mary invited us to come to Biloxi for a Sunday dinner. At the end of the dinner, as we were leaving, she handed Drago forty $100 bills, all rolled up in her hand. She said, 'Just take it. Don't worry about returning it right away. Just pay everything else and return it to me when you can. If this isn't enough, let me know, and I might be able to give you a little more.' She was a terrific model for me, and I think my boys learned a lot from her, too. We worked hand-in-hand with each other."

As a symbol of appreciation for Mary's financial and emotional support, Drago and Klara displayed for more than fifty years a large mural of Back Bay Biloxi on the back wall of their restaurant in Metairie. The portrait includes an image of Uncle Dominic Cvitanovich's Biloxi fishing camp and his Sanitary Oyster and Fish Company, where a casino now stands.

"I'm sure as proud as Drago was, he didn't want anybody to know that they had run out of money and probably wanted to keep it quiet," said Bobby Mahoney, Mary's son, who owns and operates the family restaurant in Biloxi today. "But he always knew he could talk to Mary, and she simply told him, 'I'll give you everything I've got.' That story gives me goosebumps."

"Mary Mahoney was at the top of the world with her personality," Drago's nephew David Cvitanovich Jr. said. "She could get along with an alligator catcher; she could get along with a snake; and she could get along with Queen Elizabeth. She was just the ultimate diplomat, and what a legacy she left."

As opening day drew closer, both Drago and Klara, beaming with pride for the opportunities afforded them in their new land, became

Mary Mahoney—Drago's first cousin who was the queen of the restaurant business on the Mississippi Gulf Coast—gave Drago and Klara last-minute seed money ($4,000 in rolled-up $100 bills) – to open their Metairie restaurant in 1971.

naturalized American citizens. In addition to their love for the United States and its freedoms, there was another practical reason for the timing of the citizenship ceremony: In order to obtain a permit from the Louisiana Alcoholic Beverage Control Board to sell beer, wine, and liquor at a restaurant, the business owner was required to be a U.S. citizen.

Drago had his citizenship ceremony two months ahead of Klara in 1970, shortening his legal name from Dragomir to Drago. He was one of seventy-five people who appeared before U.S. District Judge Edward Boyle Sr. The largest group of new Americans—more than 25 percent—were newly arrived from Fidel Castro's Communist regime in Cuba. Before taking the oath of allegiance from Nelson Jones, chief deputy clerk of the U.S. District Court, C. Allen Hennesy, representing the New Orleans Bar Association, talked to the group about the obligations and duties, as well as the benefits, of citizenship.

When Klara got her citizenship papers, U.S. District Judge Fred

Cassibry stepped down from the bench and shook the hand of each new citizen.

Drago's nearly half-century of struggle for freedom and for self-determination — his harrowing escapes and brushes with authoritarian intimidation, his perseverance in the face of the unknown — all flashed before his eyes as he officially became an American.

"We did a good thing," Drago told Klara.

In February 1971, Drago and Klara christened their American dream "Lakeside Seafood Restaurant" — still the original name on file with the Louisiana Secretary of State's office. Drago and Klara legally could not use "Drago's" in the original name, Klara said, for several years because of ties to the original restaurant in Lakeview. But the name and the driving force of the Metairie restaurant had Drago's written all over it.

"Almost from the beginning, everyone was calling us 'Drago's'" Klara said.

It would officially become "Drago's" soon enough.

The untold story about the Drago's Lakeside Seafood sign is that Drago didn't have enough money at the time to run another electrical line to light it up — so he simply had an electrician run a wire from the old sign. Teenaged Tommy was at his side.

9
After a Lifetime of Preparation, Instant Success

Lakeside Seafood Restaurant may have been plopped down in the relative boondocks and high weeds of Metairie, but the saving grace was that it was situated in the shadows of a burgeoning Lakeside Shopping Center. Somehow, on opening day in February 1971, there was a line of thirty people waiting to get in the front door.

"We were an instant success," Klara recalls. "Our business was booming from day one."

There were about thirty tables in the original restaurant, built on a fifty-by-fifty-foot footprint. The restaurant was open for lunch and dinner six days a week, but never on Sunday. That's the day the Cvitanovich family went to Mass at St. Dominic Church in Lakeview and tried to catch up, which meant Klara did the restaurant's books, made sure her kids' homework was done, and washed and folded dozens of tablecloths and hundreds of napkins for the coming week.

All the while, Klara maintained her full-time, travel agent's job at D. H. Holmes. That good-paying job was a security blanket in case the restaurant failed to take off.

The restaurant was located in such a natural, undeveloped area that it was not uncommon to see rabbits and raccoons darting about at night in the parking lot.

They were not on the menu.

What was on the menu, however, was every creative idea Drago had been cultivating for years for his dream New Orleans seafood restaurant. His masterfully produced fried oysters, including oysters on the half shell, which he personally shucked, drew heaping praise from the city's most respected food critic, Richard H. Collin, a.k.a.

"the Underground Gourmet" of New Orleans' afternoon newspaper, the *States-Item*.

Collin's first review of Lakeside Seafood for the June 12, 1971, *States-Item*—"Yugoslavs and Oysters Go Together"—was an encomium to a new New Orleans restaurant that was doing just about everything right.

"Drago has opened about five million oysters in his lifetime, by his own estimate," Collin wrote. "It should come as no surprise that his new restaurant's best dish is oysters. But the menu also ranges widely over the standard New Orleans seafood specialities and some more unusual ones."

Collin also mentioned something to file away for the future: Drago's "*tour de force* of fish cookery: the broiling of the whole fish, trout ($3.30), red fish ($3.50), both delicious and imaginative."

Could "charbroiling" be far behind?

Collin concluded: "It is heartening to find that some specialties of the old Drago's restaurant [in Lakeview] are being preserved and that there is a fine new oyster bar in an area of town which has long needed a good family seafood place."

When he was eight or nine, Tommy Cvitanovich bussed a few tables for his aunt Gloria at the Drago's Restaurant on Harrison Avenue, and his reward after "a super hard day's work" was a plate with a hamburger on one side and spaghetti and one meatball on the other.

"We used to call the meatballs and spaghetti 'balls and chains,'" Tommy recalled, laughing.

When his father opened his own restaurant in Metairie, Tommy was older and kept urging his dad to let him do more than merely clear dishes off the tables.

On opening day, Tommy recalls putting on an apron, which was "like a long dress" for him and standing on a milk crate in a small ten-by-ten-foot seafood boiling room, peeling shrimp.

"I might have been there all day and peeled two pounds, but I remember peeling those shrimp," Tommy said. "I grew up in the restaurant. I tell people all the time I'm a restaurant brat. I've done every part."

Drago eventually taught Tommy how to shuck oysters, expanding his on-the-job repertoire, but that was glamorous compared to one kitchen job assigned by his dad.

"I remember climbing up into the exhaust hood and cleaning it because we couldn't afford people to come out and clean it," Tommy said. "That's the dirtiest job in the world. It's like crude oil stuck to the wall, and you've got to scrape it off and then hose it off and pressure-wash it. There's a guy on TV with a show called *Dirty Jobs*, and he said this is the dirtiest job imaginable."

Tommy often used the far end of Drago's bar to do his homework on weeknights.

"When Gerry and I were old enough, we helped peel shrimp, shuck oysters, and clean tables," Tommy said. "It was a typical mom-and-pop operation."

On Friday and Saturday nights, when business was especially brisk in the first few years the restaurant was open, Tommy and Gerry cleaned the front of the house. That allowed the paid staff to clock out earlier, saving their parents on extra overhead.

"My mom and dad wanted them out of there as quickly as possible because they were on the clock," Gerry recalled. "The same thing with the kitchen help. At the end of the night, my mom and dad would go in the kitchen, empty the deep fryers of the grease, strain it, store it, and then clean the fryer. They would clean the grill and sweep and mop the floors in the kitchen. While they were doing that, Tommy and I were out front, flipping chairs upside down. We had linoleum floors. We'd sweep the floors and then mop. While we were waiting for the floor to dry, we'd go to the tablecloth and napkin bin and separate the napkins from the tablecloths. We'd get rid of all the cracker crumbs and wrappers and clean up the mess. Then, when the floors were dry, we'd put the chairs out and set the dining room for the next day."

And then?

"The four of us would go to the all-night laundromat in Lakeview," Gerry said. "That was only on Friday nights because Saturday was our busiest day, and we needed the napkins and tablecloths cleaned ASAP. After we closed on Saturday nights, the restaurant was closed on Sundays, so we would take the napkins and tablecloths home and put them in our washer and dryer. We probably had one hundred tablecloths and a couple hundred napkins—with one washer and one dryer at the house. You didn't even think about it. It was what you did. It was our life."

Klara got a great deal on the tablecloth material from Shushan Brothers, and her mother Marija, who was in New Orleans for an extended visit before the restaurant opened, hemmed them over several months.

"Even now, in my machine at home, I wash a few tablecloths that can't be sent out," Klara said. "During the early days of the restaurant, I always looked at the fact: could I pay all my bills? I felt very good at the end of the month when I could pay all my bills. Thank God, I was never behind."

Drago's role was to keep the oysters coming and the customers happy. Because of his ties to the community of Croatian oystermen, he developed trusted relationships with the men plying the oyster beds in south Plaquemines Parish.

"Eddie Kurtich had the best of the best oysters, and he knew the bedding grounds," Klara said. "He gave us the best of *his* best."

In between shucking oysters, Drago would make runs to Schwegmann's for supplies—Schwegmann's sold more than engagement rings!—sometimes three or four times a day when the restaurant was low on some commodity.

The back of Drago's Ford Club Wagon—the family car—doubled as the traveling oyster chest.

"He went from boat to boat to boat," said his nephew, David Cvitanovich.

"My dad would go down there in his white van—and let me tell you, over many, many trips, it was ripe in there," Tommy said. "That was in the old days, when it wasn't unusual for oysters to just sit on the deck for a day or two and then be tossed in an unrefrigerated van coming back here. The oyster companies used to have those flatbed trucks. They'd load the oysters up on a flatbed and drive them in and then put them in a cooler. We would unload the van and load them in our walk-in cooler. Today, there are all kinds of rules from harvest to refrigeration—and rightfully so—which were needed."

The new regulations ensure that oysters served raw on the half shell are safe to eat, Tommy said.

"Once that oyster comes out of the water today, it needs to be

With decades of hands-on experience, Drago was an expert in combing through a pile to find the best oysters. He could find the best of the best.

in refrigeration," Tommy said. "And not only does it need to be in refrigeration, it has to be in a certain cooler where the temperature of the product and the temperature of the cooler are going down a certain amount each hour. That's why you don't hear about a lot of people getting sick anymore. That's because the state's Wildlife and Fisheries and the Board of Health are definitely doing their job. And technology has finally caught up with good practices. We've come up with a protocol and plan, and we're doing things the right way."

Back in the 1970s, all Drago had were his van, his oystermen contacts, and his lead foot. Relatives and friends said Drago wasn't the greatest driver, but he managed to get from point A to point B without causing too much collateral damage.

Drago also was a master of improvisation. On one of his pre-dawn oyster runs to south Plaquemines Parish in the mid-1970s, Drago was driving back home loaded with twenty-five sacks of oysters when his station wagon's windshield defroster stopped working and the glass kept fogging up on the inside. There was nothing Drago could do to clear his line of sight.

You can't get much fresher than this!

"He got so frustrated he took his toupee off and wiped the window, and then he threw the toupee out of the window—and he never wore it again," said attorney Albert Nicaud, who waited tables at Drago's while getting his undergraduate degree at the University of New Orleans and then pursuing his law degree.

But Drago knew one thing: oysters put money on the table, and he began teaching Tommy the subtle nuances of what is a very exacting and potentially dangerous craft.

"Actually, today, I would rather clean bathrooms than shuck oysters," Tommy said. "Cleaning the hood was once every two or three months. I'll grab a mop today before I grab an oyster knife."

Tommy began opening oysters seriously when he was a student at Archbishop Rummel High School.

"It's a learned trade, and you've got to practice," he said. "It's not something that comes easy. Experience will show you where the sweet spot is and where to put the knife on it. You want to wedge the oyster into the lead [brace] so that if the knife slips, it will go into the lead rather than into your hand. I've got one good scar. I've probably been to the emergency room at least a dozen times with oyster knife cuts. I even had to be admitted to the hospital once due to an infection from an accidental oyster stab wound. As much as it has paid so many bills, all I have to say is, 'God bless the oyster shuckers!'"

And, Tommy might add, God bless the back of the house.

The success of so many great New Orleans restaurants often rests on the ingrained skills of anonymous chefs who are able to create masterpieces with a spoon, a spatula, and an imagination.

Drago and Klara moved heaven and earth to allow their quiet stars in the back of the house to shine. People like "Mama Ruth" Jenkins, Anna Thomas, and Freddie McKnight.

Klara and Drago never learned from a culinary school textbook or an MBA curriculum how to create a successful restaurant in New Orleans, but they knew one thing: the back of the house is where the sizzle explodes.

10
Back of the House

Great food — every single time — is the unquestioned foundation of an outstanding restaurant.

Drago and Klara Cvitanovich knew innately that the magic that produces a restaurant's success begins in the kitchen.

And, if a tunnel-visioned Croatian was going to bet his life's savings on forging his own American dream, he was going to put his hard-earned money on a sure thing, the culinary daily-double of two, homespun cooks, "Mama Ruth" Jenkins and Anna Thomas.

Mama Ruth Jenkins, left, and Anna Thomas were the twin stars in the Drago's kitchen. Their cooking genius was responsible for much of the restaurant's instant success.

Behind the swinging kitchen doors that separate the magic from the paying customers, Mama Ruth Jenkins and Anna Thomas went about their craft inconspicuously. Their cooking genius was stoked not at culinary institutes in New York City or Paris but on the gas stoves of their modest, WWII-era apartments—Mama Ruth's in the Iberville Housing Project behind Krauss Department Store, near Canal and Basin streets, and Anna's in the Lafitte Housing Project, bounded by Orleans and Claiborne avenues.

When Drago left his job at the original Drago's in Lakeview, where Mama Ruth and Anna ruled the kitchen, he promised them that someday he would bring them over to star in his own restaurant.

"He assured them that they would have a job with him," Klara said. "When he was still working at Acme, he told them he was opening up his restaurant and they both agreed immediately. They said, 'We are going with you.' Everybody adored my Drago because he was so easygoing and friendly with them."

Drago played the role of the pied piper. In addition to Mama Ruth and Anna, several other former employees of the Drago's in Lakeview joined the man they knew as "Brother-in-Law": There was Mama Ruth's niece Audrey; Legendre, the porter, and his nephew Leon; and Mama Ruth's niece Mildred and her husband Solomon, whose job was to pick up oysters from the docks.

"We took the entire kitchen staff here," Klara said.

Mama Ruth and Anna were so important to the restaurant's operations that Drago launched a one-man transportation service for staffers who didn't have cars: every morning, he would drive to the end of the Canal Street bus line at the New Orleans cemeteries and pick up Mama Ruth and Anna and whoever else needed a ride to Metairie.

"There was no reliable bus service from New Orleans to here, so Drago picked them up," Klara recalled. "And then, at night, he would bring them home."

One of those pickups is a cherished piece of Drago's lore. Legendre, the Drago's porter, apparently had done a little too much partying the night before and missed his regular bus stop. Eventually, Legendre found himself at the end of the line at Robert E. Lee (Allen Toussaint) and Wisner boulevards. He got out of the bus, plopped himself down on the sidewalk, and took a catnap.

Knowing Legendre was late, Drago set out on a reconnaissance mission. When he finally spotted Legendre asleep on the ground, Drago ran up to him in the middle of a gathering of people waiting for the next bus.

Drago shook Legendre by the shoulders and shouted, "You SOB, why didn't you wake up on time?"

The crowd at the bus stop was startled and confused.

"All of a sudden," Klara said, "Legendre opens his eyes and goes, 'Oh, Brother-in-Law, I'm so glad to see you!' Even though they were different races, Legendre was calling Drago 'Brother-in-Law.' Everybody at the bus stop had a good laugh."

Mama Ruth was famous for her seafood gumbo, which she made without a recipe, and also for her crawfish bisque and crab cakes.

"Ruth was probably one of the best gumbo cooks ever," Klara said. "Her gumbo was amazing. No recipe, ever."

Anna could peel shrimp faster than any machine.

"She was so fast you couldn't see what she was doing, and she was bare-handed," Klara said.

Mama Ruth, the queen of the kitchen until she retired in the mid-1990s, also was the matron of a large family, and, in her life, she overcame a vale of tears.

"She had a lot of kids, and one of her sons was in jail," Klara said. "She used to sell dinners to try to bail him out. And then when he got out of jail, three days later, he was shot in front of her door. Drago knew all of this, of course, and he used to tell Mama Ruth, 'Take home anything you want for the kids and grandkids.' The only restriction was that she couldn't take home steaks. She appreciated Drago so much because he was so protective of her. He treated Ruth and Anna royally. They knew how to cook, and they were the best at it."

Attorney Albert Nicaud was a waiter at Drago's before entering law school in the mid-1980s, and he saw Mama Ruth's anonymous talent in the kitchen produce amazing things.

"She was just a natural cook," Albert said. "You could never describe her as a chef because she had no training, but everything she put out was delicious. There were no recipes for a lot of what she cooked. But she did have all of the Yugoslavian recipes written down in a little black binder."

Mama Ruth also was a woman with a mother's heart—someone who believed in the restorative potential of second and third chances.

Her grandson Larry Jenkins, nicknamed "Moonie," used to work at Drago's on the weekends. Moonie was best friends with Freddie McKnight, who was a little older and had had several brushes with the law, including a felony conviction and a subsequent arrest for possession of a handgun.

After serving his time, Freddie knew he had to do something to get his life back on track, and he asked Moonie if he might be able to persuade his grandmother, Mama Ruth, to vouch for him in getting a job washing dishes at Drago's.

"I had been looking for a job, but it was kind of hard to find one," Freddie admitted. "I got myself in a little trouble, so I had to go in front of the judge, and when I went in front of the judge, I wanted to make sure I at least had a job to show the judge I was trying to get my life together."

Mama Ruth and Moonie asked Klara and Drago to give Freddie a try, sight unseen.

"If y'all say he's a good guy, bring him in," Drago said.

Freddie said he wasn't planning on washing dishes all his life, but it's amazing how a vote of confidence could eventually change a person's life.

"Miss Klara and Mr. Drago gave me the opportunity, so I just stuck around," Freddie said. "And then, I just fell in love with the job and the people at the job, and I fell in love with Miss Klara and Mr. Drago."

On Wednesday, February 25, 1987—Freddie remembers the exact date because his son Freddie IV was born the next day—Freddie's life's work at Drago's became washing dishes. He focused on becoming the best dishwasher ever.

Mama Ruth, a large woman both literally and figuratively, cast a huge shadow in the kitchen and on Freddie's life.

"Mama Ruth was the person who kept me here," Freddie said. "She taught me a lot."

In his nearly four decades at Drago's, Freddie rose through the ranks from dishwasher, to pot cook, to kitchen manager. Not only that, in the eyes of Tommy Cvitanovich, Freddie became indispensable to the restaurant's success.

"Freddie's going to retire when I retire," Tommy says, laughing.

In the early days when Freddie had caught up on his dishwashing, Mama Ruth would call him over to her gumbo pot to begin a series of master classes that would alter the trajectory of his life. Mama Ruth knew her health was beginning to wane.

"She told me, 'Come over here, and I'm going to show you what to do,'" Freddie recalled. "We would knock out the lunch rush, and then Mama Ruth would come over and we would wash all the dishes in the front together. She'd help me wash the pots and the dishes. She was an older lady, and she was a heavy woman. She could barely move and walk. A lot of times when she was walking, she was holding on to the table."

Mama Ruth may not have known it at the time, but her grandmotherly love directed toward a wayward soul was itself doing the heavy lifting. Her affection and encouragement were bringing a dead man back to life.

"Once she had found out I had gotten into trouble and helped me get a job, she wouldn't let me go," Freddie said. "I lost my dad when I was twelve. Six months later, I lost my mom at thirteen. Mama Ruth almost adopted me. And she was tough. She told me, 'I'll beat your ass if you ever get out there and do anything stupid again.' I definitely took that to heart. You don't get many people to take young people on once they find out you've been in trouble. They feel like if you've been in trouble, you're going to stay in trouble. And they don't want their grandson hanging with you. But it wasn't like that with Mama Ruth."

Freddie said Mama Ruth was "a straight-up pot cook," and the secret of her gumbo, created in a fifty-quart pot, was the roux and the constant stirring.

"She just grabbed what she wanted, and she knew how she wanted it to taste," Freddie said. "She was getting kind of old, and she wanted to train me on how she made everything from scratch before she retired. I did write down everything she told me because it was impossible to remember it all. When she retired in the mid-1990s, I was the head pot chef at the time. Anna Thomas was a pot cook, too, but she was more like a line cook who could work the different stations—your fry station, your flat station, your grill station."

As Freddie grew up at Drago's—in more ways than one—he often put into practice the grandmotherly wisdom he received from Mama Ruth. He honors her legacy today whenever he spots a young employee struggling, either with job duties or family responsibilities. It's his way of paying back Mama Ruth for her kindness to him.

"I try to take everyone under my wing because I know they might be going through what I went through," Freddie said. "I'm willing to give anybody and everybody a second chance—everybody! I'll give you a second chance and a third chance, because you might not get it right the second time. I'll sit down and talk to the younger kids and tell them, 'It ain't easy, but don't give up. If I had given up a long time ago, I don't know where I'd be.' I tell the kids, 'Certain things may not seem fair, but you've always got somebody worse off than you. You've got a job, and you've got somebody who wants to be standing here, working. Drive down Claiborne Avenue in the city and see the people sleeping underneath the bridge, and you're not sleeping underneath the bridge! You think you have it bad. You don't have it as bad as you think you have.'"

Now in his sixties, Freddie reflects on the chaos that buffeted his confused, younger self, and he replays in his mind the whispers of an angel.

It's his "grandmother," Mama Ruth, the woman calling out from the back of the house.

"I guess maybe she saw something in me that I didn't see in myself," Freddie said. "And that's the same thing with Miss Klara and Drago. If they see something in you and know you've got potential, they will help you bring it out."

At a birthday party for Drago at Broussard's restaurant in the French Quarter, Freddie stood up from his seat at the table and shared with his restaurant family a salvation story that some had never heard.

"I wouldn't be alive today if it wouldn't have been for Drago," Freddie said.

Then he looked directly at Drago.

"You don't know what you mean to me."

Freddie was a pallbearer at Drago's funeral.

Today, the man who began washing dishes in 1987, the man

who was a pallbearer at Drago's funeral, has a daughter who is a pharmacist.

Mama Ruth Jenkins, Anna Thomas, and Freddie McKnight were such fixtures in the kitchen for decades they became true members of the Drago's family, and family sticks together.

The combination of Mama Ruth's twenty-twenty vision for Freddie—"she saw something in me that I didn't see in myself"—and Drago's and Klara's belief in the possibility of redemption would come into even clearer focus in 2005.

In the aftermath of Hurricane Katrina, which nearly wiped the city of New Orleans off the map, Freddie McKnight and his back-of-the-house crew and the entire Drago's family saw something in New Orleans that, perhaps, the city didn't see in itself.

In the spirit of Mama Ruth, they stretched out their arms and refused to let go of the rope.

11
Majoring in "Daddy"

Success ultimately comes down to hard work. A few breaks along the way are nice, but hard work is the common denominator of sustained success.

While Drago occupied himself in Metairie by shucking oysters, tending bar, and managing the thousands of details that would allow his new Lakeside Seafood Restaurant to flourish as a reliable mom-and-pop eatery, Klara suddenly was thrust into double and triple duty.

Before opening their new restaurant—during the time when Drago was working at his interim job at Acme Oyster House in the French Quarter, two blocks away from Klara's travel agency business at D. H. Holmes on Canal Street—Klara didn't have to worry about doing bookkeeping or washing tablecloths.

But after she and Drago opened their restaurant in February 1971—and Klara continued serving as the lead travel agent at D. H. Holmes—she felt the avalanche of family and expanded business responsibilities becoming too overwhelming. After finishing her day job at D. H. Holmes, she would begin her nighttime work from five to ten p.m., as both hostess and bookkeeper at the new restaurant.

Something had to give.

"I needed to be closer to the restaurant, so I gave my resignation downtown," Klara said.

D. H. Holmes wasn't going to surrender Klara without a fight. After all, she had exponentially increased Holmes' travel business over the previous several years, prompting Billy Worden Jr., son of the agency's director, to make an intriguing pitch to Klara in 1972: she could become the director of the company's new travel agency branch office at Lakeside Shopping Center, just two blocks from the restaurant.

"I told Billy I would give him five years," Klara recalled. "The good part about it was I could come to the restaurant for lunch, and then I could come back to the restaurant again at five o'clock, and work until the restaurant closed. Then, after that, I could go do the linens."

From the eyes of Klara and Drago's son Tommy, the calculus of his parents' hard work is almost impossible to measure.

"They each did it in different ways," Tommy says. "To sit here and say my mom worked more hours than my dad or my dad worked more than my mom, I can't. My dad would leave in the morning at eight o'clock, go downtown to pick up Mama Ruth and Anna Thomas, bring them here, start mopping the floors and be here until the end of the night, when he swept up. In the middle of the day, he would bring Mama Ruth home, pick up somebody else and bring them here. Then, at the end of the night, he would bring somebody else home and then go home for eleven o'clock.

"My mom would go to work at the travel agency, work there during the day, get off, come to the restaurant, work, have dinner, and then go home with my dad and do laundry. So, to say one did more work than the other or worked longer hours, I can't do that."

And now, Tommy is the one looking in the mirror.

"I used to always tell my mom and dad, 'I don't want to work as hard as you all do'—and here I am, working as hard as they did," Tommy says. "I'm enjoying life more than they did, so I've taken a step down—and maybe even two or three steps down—from where they were. But I still work a whole lot more than the average person does."

The restaurant business can suck the life out of you if you are not careful.

Tommy said he was fascinated when he heard the comments of Shirley Lee, whose family ran the Royal China Restaurant in Metairie for more than four decades and who faced the same dilemma as Klara and Drago, and, now, Tommy: how much sacrifice, in time and energy, is too much for your family?

"Shirley said something very interesting when she announced she was selling her restaurant—she said she didn't want her kids to take over the restaurant, which is totally different than I want, because

I'm going to be proud of my kids taking over the restaurant," Tommy said. "But the line that's going to stick with me is that she and her husband worked as long and as hard as they did for the last forty years so their kids could have a normal life. She missed out on soccer games, on band concerts, on graduations, on all kinds of school events. She said, 'I worked hard so my kids don't have to miss those things with their kids.' Whereas I'm working hard because I want to build this thing for my kids and so they *can* work in it."

Sacrifice and hard work are decisions. While most of Tommy's and Gerry's high school friends attended football or basketball games or went to the movies on Friday or Saturday nights, they were both working at the restaurant to help their parents.

"A lot of kids did Little League, but I didn't," Tommy admits. "We had the Gernon Brown playground two blocks from our house, but never got to join a league. We also didn't get to do things like Boy Scouts and summer camps. The restaurant was my Little League. In high school and college, I came back and waited tables. I worked my way up. I majored in 'Daddy.' I learned a lot from my dad."

Tommy and Gerry started early helping out at the restaurant. Their hard work cleaning the front of the house kept overhead down.

Gerry, eighteen months younger than Tommy, was taking the same "family business" curriculum, always available and dutifully compliant in flipping chairs, clearing tables, mopping floors, and folding napkins. Gerry gave himself two titles at the restaurant: manager of the department of sanitation and the youngest oyster opener in Louisiana. As young boys, Gerry enjoyed working the front of the house exclusively, while Tommy worked everywhere, particularly in the kitchen.

But no one, not even Klara, who in her life of so many unknowns had tried to prepare herself for every eventuality, could steel herself for what was about to happen next.

Forget about majoring in "Daddy."

Klara was about to write her doctoral dissertation on the ultimate responsibility of being a "Mommy."

12
A Mother's Love

When Klara picked up the *Reader's Digest* at the K&B checkout counter in 1974, she nearly was at her wit's end.

As a vigilant mother, she had grown somewhat accustomed to her younger son Gerry's health issues. As an infant living in frigid Vancouver, British Columbia, Gerry had experienced more than his share of colds and other illnesses. Whenever Gerry got sick, his symptoms seemed to linger longer than they should.

Dr. Slade, an English pediatrician living on the outskirts of Vancouver, was blunt in his assessment of Gerry's health.

"There's not much I can do for him around here for him because of the weather," Dr. Slade told Klara. "All this cold weather doesn't help. You should go to a warmer climate. New Orleans has a warm climate, but I think it's too damp. You probably should go to Arizona."

In 1961, when Klara and Drago got the go-ahead to quickly immigrate to the U.S., they headed not for Arizona but for New Orleans, where they had Croatian relatives who could welcome them and throw out a warm security blanket. But despite the drastic change in climate, Gerry always seemed to get sick.

In 1972, when Gerry was twelve, Klara took him to the pediatric department at a local hospital, looking for answers.

"Doctors couldn't discover for a long time what was wrong with him," Klara said. "The doctors said things like it was a phase he was going through and that there was nothing wrong with him. Another doctor said, 'There's nothing wrong with the child. It's a case of overly worried parents.'"

One day, Klara got a call from Gerry's school, Stuart Prep in Metairie.

"They told me Gerry was lethargic and sweating and had a lot of abdominal pain," Klara recalled. "I was working at D. H. Holmes, and they told me if I couldn't come pick him up right away, they were going to call an ambulance."

Klara raced to pick up Gerry and tried to make an appointment with a doctor, only to find out his office was closed. She then drove to a second physician in Lakeview, who had been eating in the restaurant the night before.

"He took Gerry's vital signs and quickly told me, 'Klara, I don't want you to go home. I want you to go straight to Mercy Hospital. I'm giving orders,'" Klara said.

After conducting a battery of tests, doctors determined that twelve-year-old Gerry had an exceedingly hyperactive thyroid. They diagnosed him with Graves' disease, a disorder of the immune system that results in an overproduction of thyroid hormones. This was very unusual, because Graves' disease usually occurs in women over forty, not in young boys.

Surgeons removed Gerry's thyroid and four small glands—the parathyroids—that are attached to the thyroid. The parathyroids were then reimplanted in the soft tissue. Gerry understood much later what had happened.

"Post-op, the reimplantation of the parathyroids did not take properly, and that gave me a lot of symptoms, the worst of which was numbness of the hands, feet, and even my mouth and nose," Gerry said. "It messed up everything else. That's why they gave me milky calcium to take. I also was on a diet of less than ten ounces of meat per week."

"It was horrible," Klara said. "He just was not doing good. Doctors were giving him more medicine and more medicine, and it wasn't working."

For the next eighteen months, nothing seemed to relieve his symptoms. Gerry's body was so out of whack that it affected his schoolwork. In eighth grade at Jesuit High School, he would get extremely tired after eating lunch, which explained why he was nearly falling asleep in his speech and general music classes in the fall and spring semesters.

"I think it was because of those symptoms that I failed those two easy classes," Gerry said.

Then, one day in 1974, Klara went to K&B. She would always leaf through the *Reader's Digest* displayed at the magazine rack to see what condensed stories were inside. *Reader's Digest* covered the waterfront in a quick, breezy fashion—history, celebrities, recipes, jokes, science, and technology.

As Klara flipped through the magazine, her eyes serendipitously landed on a brief article about the Mayo Clinic in Rochester, Minnesota, and its breakthrough treatments for thyroid gland disease.

Klara thought for a moment and said to herself, "Why not?"

"I was brave enough to pick up the phone and call the Mayo Clinic to see if I could get an appointment for Gerry," she said. "They told me it would take six months. And I told them, 'My son doesn't have six months.'"

The receptionist expressed her sincere regrets but said she couldn't help, and Klara hung up, wracked by motherly fears.

"The next night, I read the article again and picked up the name of the doctor who was in the story—his name was Dr. Cloutier," Klara recalled. "So, I looked up his number through directory assistance and got his home number and called him at home the next morning. We spoke for probably an hour. He asked me what was wrong with Gerry, and after I explained what was going on, he asked me, 'When can you bring him up here?' I told him, 'I'll be there on Monday morning at eight o'clock.'"

The Wordens at the D. H. Holmes' travel agency bolted into action, securing airplane tickets and hotel reservations for Klara and Gerry for their trip to Minnesota.

"Don't worry about anything—you just take him up there," Billy Worden Sr. told Klara.

After arriving at Mayo, physicians put Gerry through tests for the next five days.

"At the end of his examinations, they had an assembly meeting of all the doctors who had tested him, and they said, 'Unfortunately, our colleagues in New Orleans did not diagnose him correctly. They gave him way too much medication that he did not need. He doesn't have hypoglycemia. He doesn't have low phosphate. He has way too much T3 and T4 hormones.'"

Gerry recalls hearing from the doctors that the strategy his New

Orleans doctors were using to treat his hormone imbalance was basically starving him and messing things up even more.

To a teenager who had been eating minimally on doctor's orders, the prescription advice from his new team of doctors sounded too good to be true. Klara was instructed to take him immediately to Michael's Steakhouse adjacent to the Mayo Clinic and "let him eat any steak that he could handle."

"It was freaking heaven," Gerry said, relishing the memory of finally breaking his months-long fast. "It felt good. It felt great."

"And then we went to the movies," Klara said. "It was *The Towering Inferno* with Paul Newman, one of my favorite actors. It was after that movie that Gerry asked me if he could go to medical school. I don't know if it was the steak or the movie that did that, but he asked if Drago and I could send him to medical school. I said, 'It's not up to me; it's up to you. You don't have very good grades, so you need to buckle up and study. But, if you do that, even if I have to work three jobs, you will go to medical school.'"

"From the minute I mentioned I wanted to be a doctor, she never let me forget it," Gerry said. "And anytime I thought about quitting, she'd say, 'No, you said you wanted to be a doctor!' Whether you're four years old or fourteen years old or sixteen years old, if you go through a significant medical issue, you're going to be around a lot of doctors and nurses and X-ray techs and therapists. You're either going to have a really good experience or a really bad experience, and that experience is going to be dictated by the actions of a very few people. I was lucky that I had a really good experience, even with the doctors who couldn't figure out what was going on with me. Also, maybe my decision was impacted by my mom and dad being European, and they always had a lot of respect for doctors and the road they had to travel to get there. That respect was ingrained in me, too."

Many years later, after graduating from Tulane University with a degree in biology, Gerry wrote an essay for his application to the Louisiana State University School of Medicine. He pinpointed his desire of becoming a physician to the week he received expert care at the Mayo Clinic, when he was gravely sick and anxious about whether or not he would ever recover.

"When I was finally taken off of a yearlong diet, a diet which was very restrictive in nature, I made up my mind that one day I wanted to help people the way the doctors at the Mayo Clinic helped me," Gerry wrote in his essay. "That has been my inspiration ever since."

During his medical school rotations at LSU, Gerry found himself drawn to the immediacy and the high-stakes pressure of the emergency room. Even though he completed a residency in family practice at Earl K. Long Hospital in Baton Rouge, he always found himself attracted to the life-and-death realities and excitement of ER medicine.

His early years as a physician after residency included what many doctors would consider a plum position loaded with exotic perks: he served 50 percent of the time as a traveling doctor for several cruise lines and the other 50 percent doing ER work at East Jefferson General Hospital.

Some of his regular ports of call were Hawaii, Europe, and the Caribbean. Gerry got the idea about practicing cruise ship medicine after taking a trip following his first year of medical school and

Gerry's poor health as a child and into adolescence played a role in his dream of one day becoming a doctor. That dream came true in 1986 upon his graduation from LSU Medical School.

speaking to the ship's doctor. In addition to treating the normal bumps, bruises, and sunburns that befell cruise ship passengers, Gerry also dealt with engine room accidents, kitchen accidents, respiratory infections, and cardiac emergencies, an average daily caseload of twenty to thirty patients.

"Any ship of over 1,500 passengers has two doctors, so you would work every other day, which means that every other day you were on vacation," Gerry said. "And the day you worked, the clinic was only open three hours in the morning and two hours in the evening. It wasn't all fun and games—you had your share of bad stuff happening—but it was fairly easy work."

On one of his memorable cruises, Gerry successfully treated the captain of the *SS Constitution* for an acute myocardial infarction.

"Needless to say, I got a stellar introduction at the captain's cocktail party the next time out," Gerry said.

The *Constitution* happened to be the same ship Klara had toured in the early 1950s when she was a teenager in Dubrovnik. When Gerry first mentioned to his mother that he would be working on a ship called the *Constitution* out of Hawaii, she immediately made the sign of the cross and said in Croatian: "In the name of the Father and of the Son and of the Holy Spirit."

With Gerry serving as the *Constitution*'s doctor, Klara and Drago joined him on a cruise in late 1989.

"On the first night of the cruise, my mom won a contest and was brought up to the stage," Gerry recalled. "The cruise director asked her to introduce herself and asked her if this was her first cruise. She said, 'No,' and then she took a few minutes and told the story of the first time she was on the *Constitution* in Croatia. It was funny because the cruise director was surely expecting a five-second answer, but the way she told the story was incredible. The cruise director, Doug Donnell, was really enthralled and so was the entire audience in the theater. Obviously, she was a celebrity that week. I recall being very proud!"

When Gerry was back home in Metairie for a month or two, he would make a 180-degree pivot in terms of stress levels, filling his schedule with as many ER shifts as he could manage—sometimes forty or fifty in a two-month period.

"That was like doing four months of work in two months," Gerry said.

Interestingly enough, he found many of the skills that he relied on as an ER doctor were things he learned directly as a waiter in his parents' restaurant.

"When you're in the ER, you have a certain number of rooms for patients, and there are patients in different stages of care," Gerry explained. "Some people are waiting to see the doctor, some have already seen the doctor, some are waiting for tests, some are waiting for procedures or X-rays, some waiting for discharge. In the restaurant, as a waiter, you have a similar scenario. You have your station of tables, you have some people who have been just seated, others who have ordered and are waiting for different stages of their dinner, and even others who are waiting for their bill. In both scenarios, you need to have a multiple-track mind. It's your job to manage that situation and keep things moving along. You're also responsible for people leaving satisfied.

"One of the biggest things is delays in care. In the restaurant business, you can check three boxes on every customer: you have to serve good food, you have to be nice, and you have to be fast. If you don't check every box, you're hurting yourself. In health care, the first three boxes are the same. If you don't check all three boxes, people may not come back. You have to be good, nice, and fast."

Gerry was out to dinner at a New Orleans restaurant recently with Klara, his daughter Maya, and his son Drago when Klara started to show signs of distress that she had some food caught in her airway.

"Mom, can you talk?" Gerry asked from across the table.

When she didn't respond, he got up quietly and repeated the question. There were people close by at the next table, and Gerry apologized for what he was getting ready to do next. He cupped his hand, placed it in the middle of Klara's back and then struck the hand to send air toward her windpipe. After a couple of whacks, the food went down and Klara cleared her throat with a glass of water.

"Just relax, Mom," Gerry said as the crisis passed.

"I walked around to my seat and I sat down, and I could see my kids' eyes were wide open," Gerry said. "I said, 'All right guys, what do I always tell you about the number one rule in an emergency situation?' And my daughter Maya says, 'Take your own pulse.' The rule is from a crazy book I read in med school called *The House of God*. Rule number one in *The House of God* is this: 'In an emergency situation, the first thing to do is to take your own pulse.' What it means is that in those situations, you need to keep calm and don't let your heart race or get nervous. If you're the captain of the ship and you panic, how can you expect everyone else to keep their stuff together? So, when you're running the show, when you're in charge, even when you don't know what to do, don't panic."

In 2014, Gerry was dining with a coworker at a restaurant on Metairie Road and was walking to the bathroom when he suddenly heard a commotion in the dining room. He walked out and saw several people standing around an elderly woman. She had food

Little Drago Cvitanovich, Gerry's youngest son, wore a family christening gown that was more than one hundred years old at his baptism in 2007 at St. Patrick's Church in New Orleans.

stuck in her airway and couldn't breathe. By the time Gerry walked up, she was in severe distress.

"They were trying to do the Heimlich maneuver, but they weren't having any success," Gerry said. "I asked the people there to step aside since I was a doctor."

After assessing the woman's condition, Gerry performed the Heimlich maneuver successfully and put the lady back down into her chair. He knelt down next to her while she was huffing and puffing and trying to catch her breath.

"Who . . . are . . . you?" the lady asked between gasps.

"My name is Dr. Cvitanovich, and you're going to be fine now."

The woman suddenly stopped gasping, sat straight up, looked at Gerry and said: "I know your mother!"

"I loved being an ER doctor," Gerry said. "I wasn't the best ER doctor in our group from a technical perspective, but I was very compassionate and communicated well, which is what built me a good reputation."

Gerry relied on that good reputation in 2003 when he rolled the dice and decided to enter the urgent care field, opening the first of a series of urgent care centers that he eventually sold to Ochsner. In 2013, he ran successfully for Jefferson Parish Coroner.

"Not to toot my horn too much, but I was very successful as a practicing physician, and I've been successful in elected office as well, but I was extremely successful in the business of health care," Gerry said. "Furthermore, Tommy is extremely successful in the restaurant business. It's not a coincidence that both of us, in completely separate businesses, have been significantly successful. A lot of that is the lessons you learn through osmosis. We never sat down in a classroom where my mom and dad taught us this or that. They never even said, 'We're teaching you this.' You just learn stuff. In retrospect, I think the best thing they taught us was how to treat people right.

"My dad told me a long time ago: 'Look at people and how they treat somebody who can't do something for them. That will tell you everything about that person.' One rule of thumb for me is, 'How do people treat the person serving them in a restaurant?' If they treat the waiter like crap, that tells you a lot more about them than whether they are nice to you or not. Whenever I think of that, I think of my dad."

One thing is certain, had Klara not picked up that *Reader's Digest* one day at K&B and if she did not have the nerve to pick up the 300-pound telephone and make not one, but two phone calls to ask for medical help from total strangers, Gerry's story may have had a different ending.

She had a mother's love. She had spunk.

"I do have spunk," Klara said, "because I did not want to lose my son."

13
Mom and Pop

It didn't take long for Lakeside Seafood Restaurant to capture both the palates and plaudits of its paying customers and local food critics.

Just four months after opening in February 1971, Richard H. Collin, the anointed Underground Gourmet of the *States-Item,* placed Drago's on his "can't-miss" radar screen, creating a word-of-mouth buzz more effective than any advertising campaign.

From Collin's perspective, it was easy to see why the mom-and-pop restaurant was thriving: delicious seafood at a great price.

When Collin next wrote about the restaurant four years later in August 1975, it had now become officially known as *Drago's* Lakeside Seafood Restaurant, finally adopting the family name after Drago's in Lakeview had closed. Business in Metairie was booming to the point where Drago and Klara were in the midst of their first ambitious expansion of the building's original footprint, which measured approximately fifty-by-fifty feet.

Collin was effusive in his praise. The review from the city's most respected food critic was something money could not buy. Collin wrote:

> The changes now taking place at Drago's Lakeside Seafood Restaurant will completely transform the physical appearance of Fat City's pioneer seafood and oyster restaurant. The premises and exterior facade will be more than twice as large when the renovations are complete.
>
> Even more impressive, however, are the less-obvious changes that have already taken place in Drago's kitchen. There has never

been any doubt that this was a good seafood restaurant. But now, with success apparent, Drago's has become more professional and more assured about what it is doing, especially in the kitchen.

When the complete renovation work is completed in November [1975], Drago's will also unveil the first Yugoslavian kitchen in New Orleans, with eight authentic specialties joining the excellent array of standard New Orleans seafood dishes already on the menu. This is fitting, since seafood and Yugoslavs have gone together since the Yugoslavs began emigrating to this area from Dalmatia in the early part of this century. Oysters, of course, are native to Louisiana and Gulf waters, but modern cultivation techniques responsible for the abundance of oysters we enjoy, as well as the special salty flavor of our Plaquemines oysters, were all innovations introduced by Yugoslavs.

Collin singled out the locally sourced oysters on the half shell ($2.30 a dozen). Remember, these were 1975 prices! Collin continues:

> The *piece de resistance*, however, is the giant soft shell crab dinner (highly recommended) which overflows the plate at $5.50 (highly recommended). Or better still, order the excellent seafood platter (highly recommended) which is one of the handsomest and most delicious in town. Its star is the grand and perfectly fried soft crab, which has the crispness and nutty flavor that only perfectly fried crabs consistently exhibit. But the fried oysters (highly recommended), the fried shrimp (highly recommended) and the fried fish (highly recommended) all hold their own. . . . This is a classic seafood platter beautifully done.
>
> Just as good is the excellent broiled flounder (highly recommended), beautifully scored, nicely buttered and delicious, at $3.65. Drago's is also expert at the rare art of whole-fish broiling, with trout and redfish featured. It's good to see a restaurant grow and not rest on its laurels.

Two things immediately stand out from Collin's 1975 review.

First, Drago and Klara were unafraid to make an educated gamble that their New Orleans seafood-centric menu could be enhanced, and not diminished, by the addition of exotic Yugoslavian dishes, which Collin described as "platonic" but which were largely unknown to people growing up in the 504.

Second, the "rare art" of whole-fish broiling might be considered a precursor to other fish-grilling techniques that Drago's subsequently made famous, in which the scaled skin of the fish is plopped on an open grill and a savory butter, garlic, and cheese sauce is added to marinate and smoke in its "natural" serving dish.

Drago and Klara viewed the addition of Yugoslavian dishes to their menu as a step forward and also as a way of casting a wider net.

"Our original menu was mostly seafood, and we had pork chops and chicken," Klara said. "Steaks were not that big for us in those days. But I remember people of Croatian and Eastern European origin would come in and talk to us and they would ask, 'Why can't you make something my grandmother made for me many years ago?' So, we decided, 'Let's try some Yugoslavian dishes.'"

Through her contacts with the Croatian consulate to the U.S., Klara tracked down a chef named Dusanka, who had been head chef of a major hotel in Belgrade before immigrating to Chicago.

"She couldn't move down here forever, but she was willing to help us once a month to teach me and a couple of other people the dishes we were pushing," Klara said. "She taught Mama Ruth, but she also gave me written instructions. Then, Richard Collin took over—'the best this and the best that!'"

In 1976, Collin tossed out more kudos: "This might well be the best seafood restaurant in town. Drago's has always been good; every year it seems to get better. This past year has been an extraordinary one for Drago's. The restaurant is now much larger, the parking is adequate, and the menu is sheer poetry."

The following year, Collin raved about the expanded menu and once again wrote glowingly about the sophistication with which a South Louisiana kitchen—5,700 miles from Dubrovnik—could reproduce the delicacies of the old country.

Collin's January 22, 1977, Underground Gourmet column could not have been more glowing about all things Yugoslavian. The headline declared: "Drago's Lakeside: Addictive Yugoslavian Cuisine."

Collin got right to the point: "Drago and Klara Cvitanovich have created a showplace for a fascinating European culture with cuisine to match. For their genius and excellence in the kitchen, they have my deepest appreciation."

He noted that Drago's had been "one of our best seafood restaurants" since it opened in 1971 and had gotten even better. Drago's served, he wrote, "one of the best seafood gumbos in town" (a silent shout-out to the anonymous kitchen matriarch Mama Ruth!), and he crowned its fried soft shell crab as a "platonic dish."

But what caught Collin's enlightened eye and taste buds were eleven Yugoslavian entrees—not "just one or two exotic dishes"— and the biggest surprise was that "a major showcase of Yugoslavian food in America is to be found in our own Fat City." He described the *musaka* (made with ground beef and veal cooked between layers of eggplant and served with sour cream) as both a "platonic dish" and a "*tour de force* of sheer delight."

"The crust on top is not pastry but [the] eggplant [is] so crisp it resembles pastry," he said.

Other Yugoslavian favorites of Collin were the *cevapcici* (ground beef and lamb with onions shaped like sausages); *raznici* (grilled pork and veal); *muckalica* (cut-up pork tenderloin grilled with green peppers and onions); and *riblja marinada* (marinated fish).

Collin said the *musaka* and *riblja* were so "rare in conception and taste" that "it makes me feel like simply getting up in the restaurant and applauding."

He also branded the fried squid, served as an appetizer but in enormous portions, and the *punjena lignje* (baked stuffed squid with rice) "platonic dishes."

"I knew that this was a good restaurant—it's well on the way to becoming a great restaurant," Collin concluded. "Bravo and *zivjeli* (cheers)."

"The stuffed squid was a lot of cutting and chopping, so it was not done that often but for celebrations," Klara recalled. "*Musaka* is primarily a Greek and Lebanese dish, but it reaches all the way to Italy. Everybody made *musaka* according to what they had to prepare. *Musaka* in Italy later turned into lasagna. Our *musaka* had layers of fried eggplant, and you mixed in the meat and covered it with milk. It all became connected. The milk tasted like cheese."

Ultimately, the gamble to add so many Yugoslavian dishes to the menu proved to be a culinary home run but a financial swing-and-miss. In many ways, Drago's was decades ahead of its time in promoting ethnic food, but it was a forward-looking decision that over the next ten years caused a fair amount of economic heartburn.

"Unfortunately, after a few years, we found out that we started losing the core of our business," Klara said. "Today it might be different, but back then, if you had a party of ten people going out to dinner, you would never get them in an ethnic restaurant. Maybe you could do that with an Italian restaurant, but nobody knew anything about Yugoslavian restaurants. People go out to eat seafood or steaks or Italian cuisine. We had some great American food, but now we were being promoted as the best Croatian restaurant in the area. It was both a blessing and a curse."

Tommy said the push by his parents to serve ethnic food was valiant because it was an indication they were always open to making changes and adding a white-tablecloth feel that might lead to even greater success. He recalls the menus in the late 1970s, with the left side listing the Louisiana-style seafood dishes and the right side listing the exotic Croatian offerings.

"It was just like the Asian restaurants—number one, number two, number three," Tommy said. "Number four was *cevapcici*, number five was *raznici*, number nine was *musaka*, and number ten was *pileci paprikas* (chicken stew)," Tommy said.

For a neighborhood seafood restaurant that had made its mark serving New Orleans-style sandwiches, po-boys, fried shrimp, fried oysters, some boiled seafood and gumbo, the addition of the Yugoslavian recipes was a sea change that lasted from the mid-1970s to the early 1990s.

"But then we started getting away from that because our business was dropping off," Tommy said. "I remember someone saying, 'There's a whole lot more people here who go out to eat seafood than go out to eat ethnic food, much less Yugoslavian food. That's a line I started using a lot on my parents. We started slowly taking things off the menu. People today say we should add some of the dishes back. It's funny. Some people will come in and say, 'You don't have the *musaka* on the menu anymore?' The reason we don't have it on the menu is because some people wait seven years to come back to the restaurant! Every now and then my mom gets this wild hair that she wants to cook *musaka* and stuffed cabbage again. No. We've already learned that lesson. I laugh and tell her, 'You want to make it? Make it and invite people to your house.'"

As emotionally attached as Klara and Drago were to their native cuisine, they also could look at the declining numbers in their restaurant and foresee a day of reckoning: would they keep the restaurant going by pumping their savings into rescuing the bottom line or would they sell it and allow their children to seek other opportunities in businesses that did not require twenty-four seven attention?

In the mid-1990s, Gerry was prospering in his field of emergency medicine, but the restaurant, if not yet on life support, simply was not flourishing as it once had. In 1995, the family held an emergency meeting during a Disney World vacation.

"I remember all of us talking about closing, and me going to work in home health care," Tommy said. "I was already doing some things in home health care. We talked about shutting down the restaurant because we were going through mom and dad's life savings. And my mom said, 'We're going to give this one, last college try.'"

Things were so fragile that, in 1993, Gerry had to lend $30,000 from his growing medical practice to keep the restaurant going.

"I recall Drago, Klara, and Tommy sitting at a booth behind the bar talking about whether or not they were going to close the restaurant," said attorney Albert Nicaud. "This was when they had the Yugoslavian food on the menu. I tell Tommy to this day, 'You were ahead of your time.' Now, there are so many different types of ethnic food[s] that people would be all into eating Croatian food and finding out what it's all about. Miss Klara has told me since then that had they not owned the building, they may not have made it because they wouldn't have been able to pay a lease."

In 1995, things still looked very bleak.

Albert said Tommy told his parents if the restaurant was going to survive, he felt it needed major aesthetic updates, moving away from its 1970s-style earth tone colors and bulky chairs. The restaurant was moderately renovated that year, updating the bar, installing a new entrance foyer, and implementing an electronic "POSitouch" point-of-sale system to better track and process orders and calculate bills.

"It was about $150,000 to renovate, and that was a lot of money for them, but basically, they said, 'We're going to invest in this,'" Albert said.

A more extensive renovation came in 1997, when the dropped ceilings were removed and a huge grill for charbroiled oysters—a dish that still was somewhat of a unrecognized treasure—was moved to the front of the house where patrons could see and smell the magic happening as soon as they walked in the front door.

But in 1995, little did anyone in that Disney World condo know that the pearl of great price—the pearl with the power to change everything, the gem of an oyster dish dreamed up in front of a fire-spewing gas grill by Tommy one day in the 1980s, almost by accident, and which in the ensuing thirty years would be shared and imitated across the world—was hiding in plain sight.

The charbroiled oyster would change everything.

14

"Star Was Born"

This is a classic "whodunit" tale. The only exception is that everyone knows "whodunit."

Tommy Cvitanovich invented the charbroiled oyster. We just don't know exactly *when*. Not even Tommy is 100 percent sure.

Over the last four decades, the charbroiled oyster—a raw oyster, resting with its natural juices in its shell, placed on a flaming grill, basted with butter, garlic, and parmesan and Romano cheese—has become universally acclaimed as one of the single-best bites of food in New Orleans, largely responsible for sparking the explosive growth of the Drago's restaurant empire over the last three decades.

In the pantheon of the Crescent City's culinary treasures, Drago's charbroiled oyster is a one-bite, calling card that immediately identifies a great New Orleans restaurant. Think of Oysters Mosca, Manale's BBQ shrimp, Antoine's oysters rockefeller, Brennan's bananas foster, Paul Prudhomme's blackened redfish, Arnaud's shrimp remoulade, Clancy's smoked soft shell crab, Galatoire's crab ravigote, Willie Mae's double fried chicken, Central Grocery's muffuletta, Leah Chase's gumbo z'herbes, Café du Monde's beignets, and Commander's Palace's bread pudding souffle.

The only question is this: *when* did Tommy first actualize his hare-brained idea of putting a raw oyster in its shell on a grill?

Like most good detective stories, the accounts differ and are hard to pinpoint accurately through the fog of time. What we are left with is the "preponderance of evidence." Luckily for New Orleans gourmands and non-lawyers, the comforting news is that despite their unknown origin and timetable, charbroiled oysters are with us

Betcha can't eat just one!

now, comforting and making everyone thankful for Tommy's fearless experimentation and serendipity.

Everyone seems to agree on the possible reason for Tommy's first experiment: In the early to mid-1980s, south Louisiana had a series of raw oyster scares. In 1982, there were 400 cases in Louisiana of people contracting gastrointestinal illness after having eaten raw oysters. Sales of raw oysters were cut in half. The state moved quickly to temporarily close oyster beds in lower Barataria Bay of Jefferson and western Plaquemines parishes, as well as in parts of lower Terrebonne Parish.

Even though those beds reopened in January 1983, the public's growing concern over consuming raw oysters triggered a large drop in sales. Additional scares regarding excessive bacteria counts followed in December 1983 and into 1984.

"We thought, what are we going to do? We might as well close," Klara recalls. "We were a shucking house, and we were also known as an oyster house. Our business was so bad you could shoot a cannon and hit nobody in the dining room."

Tommy's wheels began to turn. He already had perfected a dish called "Drumfish Tommy"—not named after himself but after Baton Rouge Shrimp Company executive Thomas Lusco who gave him the idea—in which the redfish was placed, skin and scales down, on the grill and then basted with garlic butter sauce.

Klara said she also knew that every year around Thanksgiving, regular customers who were preparing their oyster dressing and gumbo for a family feast would drop by Drago's to ask if they could have some of the excess oyster water to use for their own recipes.

"That told me that oyster water had some value to it," Klara said.

Sitting in a nearly empty restaurant, Klara, Drago, and Tommy talked about what they might be able to do to overcome the perceived safety challenges of serving raw oysters.

Tommy thought about his conversations with Lusco, who had suggested placing the drum fish scales-down on the grill and basting it with the butter-garlic sauce.

"I cut the rib part off and left the belly flap in the fish, and in that belly flap I would put in crabmeat stuffing," Tommy said. "So, then, you would have the crabmeat stuffing and the fish all in one great dish. We cooked it over the grill and then put it under the broiler to brown the top. It was about a ten- to twelve-ounce fillet with the skin and scales which acted as a second plate. The second plate holds all the natural juices and bastings. It's a very juicy and flavorful taste, and then you add a little bit of smoke from the fire. I named it Drumfish Tommy because Tommy Lusco gave me the idea."

One day, Tommy put two and two together. He was always thinking of "Drago-tizing" certain recipes, but this idea was really bizarre.

"I'm thinking, well, the butter garlic sauce that goes on the drumfish is really good, and we could see the natural juices being a part of it," Tommy said. "I also knew that oyster water was the best thing to cook with. I wondered, 'What would happen if I took an oyster on the half shell and put the butter garlic sauce on it?' I would get the natural juices of the oyster, I would get the butter and the bastings, and I would get that smoked flavor. The shell would act as a second plate, just like the scales did for the drumfish. I said, 'I wonder what would happen?'"

Tommy's memory is not crystal clear about what happened next. He does remember taking the charbroiled oyster to his mom and dad.

"Everybody's initial reaction was, 'This is freakin' good!'" Tommy recalls. "My initial thought is that we might be able to get an extra five dollars a dozen for it!"

Among the early taste-testers was a Drago's regular, Jefferson Parish Councilman Bob DeViney, a close family friend.

"Bob got to try a lot of our 'firsts' like our seafood pasta," Tommy said. "Bob and Ron Passons [another friend from the Mardi Gras Krewe of Argus] used to call the things I asked them to try 'stuff.' They both said, 'This stuff is good!'"

Klara was even more succinct.

"Star was born!" she said.

Tommy said one of the keys to the charbroiled oyster recipe is using margarine instead of butter.

"The reason we use liquid margarine is because margarine has a much higher burning temperature," Tommy said. "It's the same flavor, the same taste, but a higher burning temperature. Butter burns a lot, and the hotter the grill, the faster it cooks. In the first few weeks, we tried a few different ways. We tried to put a little wine on it. We tried it with the cheese and without the cheese, with cheese and wine. After lots of experimentation, we decided, 'Nope, it's just butter, garlic and cheese.'

"There's a lot of things you can argue about who did something first, but charbroiled oysters are mine," Tommy said with a smile. "Think about all those famous New Orleans dishes from famous restaurants. A roast beef po' boy can be from anybody. Red beans and rice, and shrimp creole can be from anybody, but charbroiled oysters are from Drago's. That's one of the few things nobody argues about. I love telling people that in Philly, there's a huge debate between Geno's and Pat's regarding who invented the philly cheesesteak. There is no such debate in NOLA."

The real argument—and it's a juicy one—is exactly *when* the charbroiled oyster moved from the status of "great bite of food" for a select group of family and friends to a regular place on the Drago's menu. And that's where the story gets really fun, with several former long-time employees and family members sharing colliding accounts.

Tommy dates the charbroiled oyster officially appearing on the Drago's menu to 1994 or early 1995. But two long-time Drago's waiters—local attorney Albert Nicaud and Dr. Ronnie Lahasky, who practices internal medicine in Abbeville, Louisiana—say the charbroiled oyster was invented and served much earlier.

"This is like the Zapruder film," Lahasky said of the mysterious timeline. "I actually think one of these oysters shot JFK, if I remember all the details from the grassy knoll."

Lahasky was waiting tables in 1985, saving money for medical school, when he remembers Tommy coming up to him with a platter of food.

"It was a Wednesday at about four o'clock, and we were setting up our tables," Lahasky said. "Tommy came up to me with a platter and said, 'I want you to try this.' And I said, 'What is this?' and Tommy said, 'Just eat it.'"

It was the first charbroiled oyster Lahasky had ever tasted.

"I remember it so well because I tell this story to a million people," Lahasky said. "I saw where Tommy was quoted as saying the charbroiled was invented in the early 1990s. I'm 100 percent sure it was the mid-1980s, because when I started medical school, I didn't work at Drago's anymore. I only worked there from 1984 to 1986. I'm going to spot you 1985, because it was sometime in that time frame. There's no doubt, because on that Wednesday night, when he gave it to me, I said, 'Man, this tastes good.' He told me, 'We're going to start selling them,' and I asked, 'When?' and he said, 'Tonight!' That is a 100 percent recollection in my mind."

Lahasky said as a waiter who loved to give diners advice, he jumped at telling them about the intriguing, new dish.

"I would go up to people's tables and I would say, 'Y'all want some oysters?' and more than likely it was the women at the table who would say, 'Oh, I don't eat oysters,'" Lahasky said. "I'd say, 'Well, we have charbroiled oysters, and they taste like steak, and I am sure you're going to eat them.' I always say it's because of me that Tommy's claim to fame is the charbroiled oyster!"

Albert Nicaud dates the charbroiled oyster to the late 1980s. Nicaud's timeline is tied to his dating history.

"I was a lawyer, and I was dating a girl at the time—the last girl I dated before I met my wife—so it must have been 1988 or 1989," Albert said. "There was a food festival that predated the French Quarter Fest called La Fete, and it was held in July in Jackson Square. My girlfriend's good friend was promoting La Fete and wanted vendors to participate and sell their wares. I told Tommy, 'This would be the ideal opportunity for you to do your charbroiled oysters and introduce it to everybody downtown and all the tourists. So, I managed to help him get a food booth in the Square that was located right by St. Louis Cathedral. I remember Tommy had four little Weber grills, and the wind was blowing in his direction all day. His eyes were burned red from all the smoke for three days. We had two boxes of Drago's business cards, and they were all gone by the end of the weekend. The line for charbroiled oysters was one-fourth around the Square."

Tommy recalls ending up in the emergency room that weekend because his eyes were so swollen from the smoke. "We were out there shucking oysters—we didn't even bring shucked oysters to the event," he said. "That was definitely early on."

Another contemporaneous piece of the evidence that Drago's launched the charbroiled oysters in the 1980s comes from a brief, unobtrusive reference in the *Times-Picayune*'s restaurant and entertainment guide from November 6, 1988. It highlighted Drago's fare as "seafood, Yugoslavian food and oyster bar, *charbroiled oysters* [italics added]."

Tommy's brother Gerry raises a valid question in the whodunit mystery: if charbroiled oysters were on menu, perhaps as early as 1988, why would the restaurant have faced such dire economic challenges in the early to mid-1990s?

Tommy says there's a compelling explanation: the initial charbroiled process was somewhat self-limited.

"For a couple of years—and this is a fact—we used to make the charbroiled by opening the oysters to order," Tommy said. "It was, 'Hey, I need a dozen!' and you had to wait for our shuckers to open them, and then I had to take them into the kitchen to cook them. The success didn't happen overnight. It wasn't like we went from zero to one hundred miles an hour. We went from zero to ten to twenty to thirty to forty and then to eighty."

How big has the charbroiled oyster business become? The demand is so great that Drago's outsources the shucking process to facilities on the Mississippi Gulf Coast, in St. Bernard Parish, and even in Alabama. The shucked oysters are transported to Metairie on platters, ready to be placed on the grill.

"We're not able to shuck the amount of oysters we need for our grill," Klara said. "We've got four positions on our oyster bar in Metairie, and we would need a minimum of eight to ten positions just to shuck the oysters we sell in Metairie. That would mean we would have to work 24/7 shucking oysters to keep up with demand. The packing house in Pass Christian has men and women shucking oysters all night long. We bring them the oysters, and they shuck them on the half shell and bring them back to us, covered in plastic containers. They come in big trays, already counted, twelve each. The vast majority of our oysters are Louisiana oysters. There are certain times of the year where we get a decent amount of Texas oysters out of Galveston Bay, which are as salty or saltier than anything you've ever had before."

Since imitation is the sincerest form of flattery, there are now hundreds of restaurants across the country that serve some version of charbroiled or chargrilled oysters.

"You can't patent a process," Tommy says. "You take that as a badge of honor."

From Tommy's perspective, the mushrooming charbroiled oyster industry is the ultimate source of pride. Tommy and his family were making a road trip through Texas recently when they got hungry and didn't want to stop at Burger King or McDonald's. They pulled into Barton Creek Country Club just outside of Austin and asked if they could get something to eat.

"So, I open up the menu, and I see charbroiled oysters on the menu," Tommy said. "I told them, 'Give me a dozen of these.'"

It was a good meal. Afterward, the club manager visited the table—"The table visit is one of the greatest tools a restaurant manager can use," Tommy says—and asked how everything was.

"Oh, it was delicious," Tommy said. "We enjoyed it. Let me ask you something. Tell me about this charbroiled dish we just had. That was pretty good."

"Oh, man, my chef is crazy. He goes to New Orleans, and they've got this restaurant in downtown New Orleans that invented this and serves it at the Hilton Hotel. He goes there all the time and he loves it. And, quite honestly, the customers here love that dish. Did you not like it?"

"No, no, it was good. Is your chef here?"

"Yes."

"Can you do me a favor and give him my card?"

Tommy said he'll never forget what happened next. The manager took one look at his Drago's business card and said, "Oh, crap."

"The manager went back into the kitchen, and all of a sudden the chef came to the table, and we talked about how good it was and how proud I was of him," Tommy said. "It was a great moment. He was so proud of the fact that I was in his restaurant. He called the owner of the restaurant, who lived in the marina area, and the owner came over to meet us. It doesn't get much better than that. That was so cool."

Bobby Mahoney, whose mother Mary Mahoney established the iconic Mary Mahoney's Old French House restaurant in Biloxi, Mississippi and also helped Drago open his restaurant in 1971, credited Tommy for hitting a culinary home run.

"It kind of blew the market up, just like Paul Prudhomme did when he came in with his blackened redfish," Mahoney said.

"I've got to take my hat off to Tommy because if Drago's had remained just a half-shell oyster restaurant, this place would have never survived," said Dave Cvitanovich, Tommy's first cousin. "But what that boy did with the oyster business, boy, he won the Super Bowl."

Tommy says Drago's buys oysters from various dealers and processors, which is a boon to everyone's business.

"We mix it around because different areas have better times of the year to get oysters," Tommy said. "The invention of charbroiled oysters has changed the whole dynamic of the oyster industry these last twenty-some-odd years because now people can enjoy oysters in a different way. It's not just fried on a po' boy or raw. It also brings up a lot of other possibilities, like, if you can charbroil them, we can do this or that with them. Now people are using oysters in a lot more

Drago with his nephew Dave Cvitanovich. Dave's father David moved from Croatia to New Zealand to Buras in 1931 to help manage the Lulich Brothers Orange Winery.

recipes. Before, oysters were an exotic protein product, whereas now it's mainstream."

The elder Drago, who made his livelihood shucking oysters, was an immediate convert to Tommy's way of turning raw product into grilled gold.

"Every day I eat a dozen," he told the *Times-Picayune* in 1998, and he always paired the charbroiled with a crisp, white Muscadet produced near some of France's most famous oyster beds.

Rocky Weigand, general manager and vice president of Coca-Cola Refreshments, has known the Cvitanoviches since the late 1980s when he was promoting his Coke products to be sold in the restaurant. He was a pallbearer at Drago's funeral in 2017.

"There are probably very few restaurants in the world that could claim they own something, and certainly, charbroiled oysters originated here, and they have ownership," Weigand said. "As I've grown in my own position with my company, I realize even more so the significance of owning something and having it as your calling card. There have been thousands of people I've encountered over the last thirty years in the industry, and they've told me, 'Oh, you know Drago's? That's the oyster place. I've heard about those oysters.' That's an incredible benchmark."

Tommy loves nothing more than good-natured competition. His close friend, Mike Rodrigue, the owner of Acme Oyster House in New Orleans, developed his own version of "chargrilled" oysters not long after Tommy's success had planted the charbroiled originals front and center on the food map in a food town. Together, Drago's and Acme sell more "charbroiled" and "chargrilled" oysters than anyone else.

"We use different cheeses," Mike said, laughing. "I tell Tommy, 'You created it. I just made it better.' He's never punched me yet. But like Tommy has always said—and he's told me this—there's enough business to go around. This is a safe spot for people who don't normally eat oysters. They'll dive into something that's chargrilled."

Or "charbroiled," of course.

Rodrigue said Tommy's genius was figuring out the right method—something that was safe. Rodrigue had some scary encounters when he tried to pair oysters with a barbecue grill back in the day.

"I remember in college we used to get sacks of oysters for a gathering and we tried putting oysters on the barbecue pit—honestly just to get them open—but they wound up exploding on occasion," Rodrigue said. "It was like shrapnel."

Through the years, Tommy learned more than he ever thought possible about how to incorporate the charbroiled grill as a focal point for his restaurant. The flames and smoke cascading through sophisticated ceiling vents produce a Las Vegas-style fireworks show, capturing kids' imaginations.

"The little children will tell their parents, 'We want to go to the flame restaurant,'" Tommy says.

But those flames and smoke also produced a scientific challenge.

"If a restaurant is going to do it, you've got to get out your pen and paper and design around that," Tommy said. "You need more oyster bar space, more walk-in cooler space, more grill space, and possibly a separate hood. There is a wow factor. That's an unbelievable amount of air conditioning going through the vent. Most restaurants

Now world-famous, Drago's charbroiled oysters were invented on a whim by Tommy Cvitanovich in the late 1980s and burst onto the New Orleans culinary scene in the early 1990s as the single-best bite in a food-crazed city.

have what they call 80 percent makeup air—the exhaust system has to pump 80 percent of outside air in, which means 20 percent of your conditioned air is going outside. Because we produce so much smoke, we need to capture that smoke and push it outside. We're about seventy to thirty. We need a special AAON unit. If you're going to do it right, you have to design your whole HVAC system around that. Otherwise, there would be too much smoke in the building. I'm always glad to help restaurateurs figure that out when they're thinking of putting charbroiled on the menu."

From those four small Weber grills in Jackson Square, the charbroiled oyster business has exploded, and it has nothing to do with shrapnel.

"I guess if all my restaurants were going one hundred miles an hour right now, we would be well over five million charbroiled oysters a year, maybe six or seven million," Tommy said. "The most charbroiled we ever sold in one day was just under 1,000 dozen, and we've done that twice at the Hilton location. It happened when LSU played in the BCS National Championship Game [in January

2020] and for the Super Bowl between the Ravens and the 49ers [in February 2013]."

Sitting in a dining room just inside the front door of Drago's in Metairie, kitchen manager Maria Abadie marveled at the more than a dozen suitcases lined up against the back wall. The luggage belonged to tourists taking Ubers or cabs either to or from Louis Armstrong New Orleans International Airport.

"These are people coming from the airport, making Drago's their first stop before going into town, or they're people wanting to eat charbroiled oysters one last time before they go to the airport and fly home," Maria said.

How delicious and addictive are Drago's charbroiled oysters? To find out, all you need to do is to conduct a focus group with the luggage.

15

Tommy Gets His Spurs

As brothers born eighteen months apart, Tommy and Gerry, each fathers of four, have a running joke with their children.

Tommy always gravitated more to his parents' restaurant business and was less drawn to his schoolwork than his younger brother, who graduated in biology from Tulane University and then earned his medical degree from LSU.

"As we got into college, Gerry was way more serious about school than I was, and I was way more serious about the restaurant than he was," Tommy says. "I was healthier than Gerry was. Gerry took to books a little better than I did. I knew in high school I was going to be majoring in 'Daddy.' It was never really a competition, and it's still not. But I will say this: He's the rich one. He's done a great job.

"I've told my kids many times: 'Look how much harder and longer I work compared to Uncle Gerry. You know what the difference is? The difference is he studied in school, and I didn't.' I don't want to say I wouldn't have changed anything. I wanted to be a restaurateur, and I love being a restaurateur. But I don't feel sorry for myself because Gerry went to college, and he studied, and he did really well, and he makes a whole lot more money than I make."

While Tommy owns the lion's share of the Drago's restaurant business, he religiously runs every major decision past both his mom and Gerry to make sure they have built a consensus.

"There are certain times we talk about something and I'm dead set on doing it and Gerry's like, 'I don't know,' and I still do it," Tommy said. "But virtually every time something major comes up, I go to him to make sure he's okay with it. I go to my mom to make sure she's okay with it. It's incredibly rare for me to make a decision that my brother disagrees with."

Gerry said he always considered himself to be a swing vote when it came to making major decisions about the restaurant.

"Back in the early '90s, I used to joke to Mom that I was the most powerful guy in this restaurant because Tommy had his thoughts and opinions, and Mom had her thoughts and opinions," Gerry said. "Drago was starting to take a step back. He was still opening his oysters and working every day and still driving and going to pick up oysters, but he was starting to leave the higher-level decisions to Tommy, Mom, and me. Tommy would talk to me on the side, and then we'd go have a meeting. They both lobbied me because I was the tiebreaking vote. I will admit that most of the time I sided with Tommy. Most of the time my job was convincing Mom to agree with him."

Local attorney Albert Nicaud, who grew so close to Tommy and Gerry during his college days as a waiter that he delivered one of the three eulogies at Drago's funeral in 2017, said Tommy decided early on that he was totally committed to the grinding restaurant lifestyle.

"Here was this big guy, who probably would've loved to have played high school football, but his family owned a seafood restaurant and Friday nights in the fall he had to be at the restaurant working," Albert said. "We played flag football on Friday afternoons at the University of New Orleans, and we had a lot of fun. But he was always about the business."

Tommy not only provided the grunt work his parents needed as a teenager and young adult, but he always had his eyes and ears open looking for the next edge or a better way of doing things. He was a natural leader. In 1983, at the age of twenty-four, he served as president of the Yugoslav-American Club for young adults with Croatian ties. He wasn't afraid to share his ideas on restaurant-building with Drago and Klara.

"I was in my mid-twenties when I was at home and probably having coffee with my parents when they finally said, 'You know, maybe what he just said makes sense,'" Tommy said. "And then, another ten years goes by, and they're saying to themselves, 'This crazy kid wants to buy a firetruck?' or 'He wants to set these beautiful

Louisiana oysters, which I picked up myself, on a freakin' fire on the oyster grill! Are you kidding me?' The important thing to understand is that this was a full-circle kind of thing. I don't want to say I argued with my mom and dad, but we debated."

One of the common trigger conversations revolved around comparison shopping. In the early 1980s, Drago's still was very much a mom-and-pop seafood restaurant, but sometimes Tommy's parents would point to bigger chain restaurants, such as Bennigan's, and ask, "Why can't we do that?"

"I would tell my mom, 'You can't compare us to Bennigan's or Copeland's because we're a mom-and-pop," Tommy said.

One of the ironies is that now, with seven Drago's restaurants spread out across Louisiana and Mississippi, Drago's is considered the seat of wisdom, the city on a hill.

"You can pick your hundreds of independent restaurants in this area, and now those owners' kids are probably saying, 'We're not Drago's, Mom!'" Tommy said. "But with that full circle comes a different set of expectations."

Klara saw in Tommy someone with an innate ability to engage any audience, whether he was talking to the kitchen or wait staff about high expectations or if he was making a pitch to restaurant industry leaders. His advice was authentic and down to earth. After all, this was someone who literally grew up peeling shrimp while standing on a milk crate in a restaurant kitchen.

"We did it together, and basically I okayed everything he asked for, but he's the one with all those great ideas about having many restaurants," Klara said. "When he went on the board with the National Restaurant Association, he was meeting every month with some of the most influential people in the hospitality business, and he was getting ideas and was getting smarter. He became a tremendous speaker even though he never took any public speaking lessons."

Tommy considers his volunteer service with the Louisiana Restaurant Association (LRA), which led to appointments with the National Restaurant Association and the Canadian Restaurant Association, essential building blocks in his career.

"I got involved by accidentally going to a meeting," Tommy said, laughing.

Jim Funk, president and CEO of the LRA from 1980-2010, invited Tommy to a New Orleans chapter meeting of the LRA in 2001, but Tommy accidentally wound up going to an LRA board meeting instead.

"I sat in that room and got the fever right away," Tommy said. "Jim Funk saw that I had the fever and appointed me to the LRA state board as an industry rep. I was on a state board before I was even on the New Orleans board. At the first LRA meeting, Dickie Brennan got up and spoke, and I was so impressed with him. Every single meeting, every single social event with the restaurant associations, I've learned something. I might not use it right away, but I put it in the back of my head and use it a month or a year later."

Sometimes it was little things that made a big difference. Dr. Ronnie Lahasky, a former waiter, remembers Tommy spearheading the redesign of the bar in the mid-1980s.

"He said, 'The bar was kind of old-fashioned, and now it looks so much better,'" Lahasky said.

Tommy always was looking at ways to inject more buzz into the business. When Crazy Johnny's Steak House nearby began offering $6.99 steak dinners in the early 1990s, Tommy got the idea of offering $9.99 lobster specials.

"Crazy Johnny's was attracting hundreds of people with their steak specials," Tommy said. "So, we did a $9.99 lobster special as a 'loss leader.' We wanted to get people in the restaurant."

His willingness to take a risk in embracing the next big thing was Tommy's calling card.

"All of a sudden, he started doing his own dishes, he started tweaking the restaurant—'Let's get rid of this and get rid of that,'" said A. J. Lulich, Tommy's first cousin. "All of a sudden, he's doing lobster, and lobsters are going through the roof, pulling people in, and then the charbroiled was the killer. He started changing things up, and all of a sudden, they were pumping money into the restaurant. All of a sudden, the carpet is fresh, the front is changing, and they get an interior designer to come in and redo stuff. That's the kind of stuff the customer likes to see."

Coca-Cola executive Rocky Weigand witnessed Tommy coming of age. Rocky was trying to capture the Drago's account for Coke—

Tommy somehow convinced Drago to buy a firetruck, and the rest is marketing history.

which included not only soft drinks but also an extensive wine and liquor list—and he finally got an in-person meeting with Tommy to pitch his proposal in the late 1980s.

"The main dining room to the left was dark and gloomy," Weigand recalled. 'The food was incredible, but it wasn't the place where you would say, 'I can't wait to go to Drago's!' It was stuck in a time capsule."

As any good sales rep knows, it's important to discern as quickly as possible who the decision-maker is in order to make the sale.

"It was clear that the person making the decisions was Miss Klara," Rocky said. "We were pitching a house brand—I think it was a Gallo product—but we couldn't get Drago's to do it. I went in and saw Tommy, and we sat at the old bar. I poured him a glass and told him the price point, and he may not have even tasted it. He told me, 'All of this sounds good. I'm good with it. The only thing you have to do now is convince my mom.' I knew his mom a little bit, but, frankly, I was a little scared of her."

Amazingly enough, Weigand eventually made the sale.

Fast forward several years. Every time Weigand met with Tommy on a sales call, Tommy would tell Rocky about his burning desire to remodel the restaurant.

"I want to get rid of these tables and chairs, pull down the wallpaper, rip up the carpet and open up the ceiling," Tommy told Rocky.

Eventually, Tommy convinced his parents that the remodeling was necessary to allow the restaurant to thrive.

Rocky grew so close to the family—especially to Klara—that he beats Tommy and Gerry to the punch in wishing Klara a happy birthday every March 1, with early-morning phone calls and strategically placed yard signs that proclaim: "Happy Birthday, Miss Klara, Love Rocky!"

Rocky credits Tommy with having an innate vision for the right time to make a move.

"What he did was the right thing to do, and, quite honestly, it catapulted the restaurant," Rocky said. "I realized early on that Tommy was going to be the driving force of creativity and sustainability, and Klara and Drago would be the foundation of resources and a sound mind in doing the right things. But, if things were going to go left or right in terms of growth, it was going to be driven by Tommy. Because of that, I also realized there were going to be home runs, triples, doubles, and there were going to be some strikeouts. Tommy could come up with some crazy ideas, but it was always done from a place in the heart: 'How can this create more jobs and help people?'"

What Gerry calls the "big renovation" of Drago's took place in 1997. He has that year fixed in his memory because in January 1997, he had rented his home in the Warehouse District during Super Bowl week to some well-heeled fans from the Boston area. They came to Drago's for dinner and had charbroiled oysters.

"I remember afterward one of them telling me, 'You know, this food's amazing and your family's great, but I'll give you my criticism: The atmosphere doesn't match the food,'" Gerry said. He was like, 'Your building is stuck in the '80s.'"

With the sales of charbroiled oysters booming, paying for the renovations no longer was an issue.

From his perspective catering to family-owned businesses across the south, Rocky Weigand said he is astounded by the tight-knit relationships exhibited by Klara, Tommy, and Gerry.

"In my industry, in particular, we deal with a lot of family-owned

Klara feeds the grandchild of her good friend, Coca-Cola executive Rocky Weigand.

companies and you hear, 'Don't listen to my brother; I run this place,' and that puts you in the middle," Rocky said. "Tommy and Gerry get along tremendously well, and they're very different people, not only from what they do for a profession but also what they like to do in their free time. I've never seen any jealousy demonstrated on either side. I've always thought that was a byproduct of Klara and Drago saying, 'We're going to be one family. We may differ and we may close the door and have a discussion that someone is going to be upset about, but when that door opens, we're family.'"

    The family atmosphere that Klara and Drago created was something that went beyond immediate family. And every Drago's employee knew it, because the patriarch of the family wanted it that way.

16

The Croatian King

Especially in his later years, the stool just to the left of the bar at Drago's was the place where nearly every patron would encounter the gentle giant—the grandfather from another generation and culture.

Drago Cvitanovich's stool was less a throne than an observation deck.

From his elevated perch, Drago would welcome regular customers, even those he barely knew or didn't know by name, with a craftily familiar, "Hello, my friend, good to see you!" and revel in the excitement of children racing toward the lobster tank or moving more cautiously toward the fire and smoke of the oyster grill.

Drago never really pontificated from his perch, unless it was getting close to quitting time, when his energy was waning. Even without the benefit of a megaphone, his Croatian baritone could fill every cranny in the first-floor dining rooms.

"We usually closed at nine o'clock, and Miss Klara was here every night, and he couldn't go home until Miss Klara went home," said Brittney Montes de Oca, who put herself through nursing school waiting tables at Drago's for years after graduating from Mount Carmel Academy and who cared for her beloved boss in the hospital near the end of his life. "If he thought people were overstaying their welcome, he would literally tell them, 'We don't serve breakfast!' He would say, 'No breakfast! No breakfast!' He would say it at the bar, but he would say it loudly enough so that people could hear him without him really talking to them. Then they would look around and say, 'Oh, gosh, we're the last table here. Maybe we should get up and go.'"

Sometimes, from his chair, he would sing, "Good Night, Irene!" People finally got his not-too-subtle message. It also wasn't unknown for Drago to flicker the lights—the universal symbol of "Please, go home, now!"

Drago was a man of work, routine, and faith. He usually would get to the restaurant at nine in the morning, work all day, and eat dinner at nine or ten at night. On Tuesday nights, when business was slow, Albert Nicaud would stand behind the oyster bar with Drago and chat. It was a master class in the virtue of perseverance.

Drago told Albert about what happened after WWII when he immigrated to Canada and received care packages from his brother and sisters in Louisiana.

"It built up to the point where he didn't want to receive any more free stuff," Albert said. "He wanted to do it on his own, and he wanted to help people the way he was helped during and after the war."

A man in love with his trade, Drago shucked millions of oysters in his lifetime.

In their Tuesday night history classes, Albert learned why Drago fell in love with America.

"His perspective was great," Albert recalls. "He came from Yugoslavia, and he was probably one of the greatest Americans that I ever knew. He loved America and what it stood for. He was the American dream, and he was strong as an ox. He was in his sixties when I worked here, and he would just pick up those sacks of oysters, which had to weigh about sixty pounds, like it was nothing."

At Drago's Funeral Mass at St. Clement of Rome Church in 2017, Albert was honored to join Drago's sons Tommy and Gerry in sharing his reflections about why he revered his boss.

"That made me feel great to be asked," Albert said. "I always say I'm the son he never wanted. Both of my parents died when I was young. My dad died in my freshman year of college, and my mom died two years after that, and I'm the youngest of nine. I put myself through school, paid for my college and law school. Drago and Klara kind of took me under their wing."

Drago taught Albert something every day. One day, a businessman in a coat and tie came into the restaurant around five in the afternoon, sat at the bar and ordered a glass of house wine from Drago.

"It was probably two dollars," Albert said. "At a table right near the bar, there was a family with a baby, and the baby was crying. Drago and I were at the bar, and this man takes two dollars out of his pocket and puts it down on the counter. He tells us, 'I just want to pay for my wine and leave. I can't stand this baby crying. I'm out.' Drago takes the two dollars and slams it back on the counter and says to him, 'Listen! I was baby! You was baby! He is baby! Babies cry! Now, get out!'"

Klara says Drago's fondest thrill was watching people come into the restaurant and then finding out they were celebrating a birthday.

"His biggest pleasure was to go out and sing 'Happy Birzzday,'" Klara said.

"If you sang 'Happy Birzzday' at the table without him, he would get mad," recalls Brittney, who tried not to make that mistake while waiting tables. "And, if you sang louder than him, he would get mad."

At the restaurant, Drago always had his eyes out for the little

There was never a time where Drago was left without a song to sing—especially when he regaled patrons with his barreling baritone version of "Happy Birzzday."

things. When he spied a napkin on the floor, he would point to it and tell a passing waiter: "Dollar bill!"

That meant, of course, if the napkin or cracker wrapper on the floor were a dollar bill, you'd pick it up.

Dr. Ronnie Lahasky will never forget the day he was carrying two glasses of water to a table and the bottom of one of the glasses broke, shattering on the floor and spilling water everywhere.

"You could hear Drago shouting, 'Ronnie! I told you to use tray! You should've used tray!'" Ronnie said. "Even though he never told me to use tray . . . I should've used tray."

"If someone dropped a glass or a plate, he'd go up to them and say, 'Hey, pretty soon, you going to owe me a case,'" Gerry said.

Going back to his times of near starvation in WWII, Drago also had an obvious pet peeve for wasting food, especially bread. Ivana Popich, who manages the front of the house, said Drago always told his waiters "not to waste the bread."

"That goes back to him being in the war and not having bread," Ivana said.

As a lovable grandfather with an infectious sense of humor, Drago also gladly accepted being on the other end of practical jokes, but after the dust settled, that usually elicited a few Croatian four-letter words.

"Drago taught a few people how to curse fluently in Croatian because his attitude was, 'God didn't understand Croatian over here. He only understood it over there,'" said A. J. Lulich, Drago's nephew. "At the same time, Drago was a mentor to so many of these guys."

One late afternoon—long before the advent of cell phones—Drago was driving on the West Bank after having dropped off a member of his kitchen staff. On his way back, he got a flat tire, and he didn't have a tire iron to remove the lug nuts.

Drago couldn't speak much English, but he knocked on the door of a modest, unassuming house where his car had rolled to a stop, and the gracious homeowner allowed him to come inside to make a phone call to the restaurant.

Albert answered the phone.

"I'm busting out laughing because I'm picturing Drago talking in broken English, having to go into somebody's house to make a call," Albert said. "He was getting frustrated at me, and he finally told me he wanted Tommy to come pick him up. I'm killing myself laughing, so I hand the phone to Tommy. Drago tells Tommy, 'Number one, fire Albert.'"

Another time, Drago was waxing poetic about the succulent Creole tomatoes Klara had grown in a small garden in their backyard in Metairie. He had several of them in a large bowl at the oyster bar, where he was shucking oysters. He would offer them to good customers, saying, "Oh, my Klara … my Klara grow them," Drago said. "Look how beautiful they are! Sweet, sweet, sweet! They are like fruit!"

"He kept going on and on about these tomatoes for maybe three or four minutes," Albert said.

Klara and Tommy were sitting in a booth near the bar. Albert gave them the eye and got their attention. He reached into the bowl, pulled out three of the tomatoes and started juggling them.

"Drago looks over at Tommy and Miss Klara and says something in Croatian, and they both fall out of the booth laughing," Albert said. "So I ask them, 'What did he say?' They say, 'He wants to know if we have enough insurance in case I kill Albert.'"

"When Tommy and I were working in the restaurant in the 1970s and '80s, a lot of the staff in the front of the house were our friends that we knew in college," Gerry said. "There was a group of those guys, including Albert, that Drago loved to hate. He hated them, but he loved them! They would drive him crazy, but he loved the back and forth. Those guys, like Albert, are doctors and lawyers and engineers now. One of the great sources of pride for my mom and dad was seeing how these people—and her grandchildren—came to work here, worked hard, and became successful or are going to be successful. Drago felt the same way. They could terrorize Drago, but he was always a good sport. That's why he said, 'Fire Albert!' all the time."

Drago probably wanted to commit bodily harm against Tommy one day in the early 1980s. There had been a fire at the restaurant, and the contractor installed a phone line behind the bar so that he wouldn't have to keep dropping coins into a pay phone attached to the wall to make or accept calls.

With the new phone line installed, Tommy had the bright idea to spend $125 on a high-tech phone that could store ten numbers on speed dial and also allow for call forwarding. The speed-dial feature would make it easier for Drago to call Tommy at his apartment. Tommy had worked late one night and, in the interest of getting some sleep, he decided to forward his apartment phone to the pay phone.

The next morning, when Drago pressed "Tommy" on the fancy speed dial phone at the bar, the pay phone rang because Tommy had forwarded his apartment phone to the pay phone. Drago hung up the fancy phone and walked over to answer the pay phone, but no one was there. This happened three or four times. When Drago speed-dialed "Tommy" again—and the pay phone rang once more—Drago was growing so increasingly flustered that he told Klara, "You go and answer it, and I will stay on the line."

Klara picked up the pay phone, and Drago heard her voice on the other end.

"So, he's furious about this phone and how much money we spent on it," Tommy said, laughing at the memory. "And, every time he can't reach me and the pay phone rings, he wants to smash it."

Drago didn't take much time off of work, but when he and Klara had some spare time, they enjoyed going to the casino to play the penny slots. He also enjoyed putting a few dollars on the Louisiana Lottery every Wednesday and Saturday, when either he would buy tickets himself or he would send someone to Breaux Mart to buy a few tickets for him.

That gave Albert a devilish idea.

"So what we did was record the lottery show from Wednesday night, and I went and bought the lottery tickets with those winning numbers the next day," Albert said. "There was a little VCR with a TV at the restaurant, and the next night, I told everybody where I was sitting with Drago, 'Come on, the lottery show's about to start.' So we plug in the VCR, and the guy comes on, 'Now, here's the winning numbers for the Louisiana Lottery!' And Drago's got his ticket. He hit the first number, and you could see his hand start shaking. And when he hit the last number it was—'I vin! I vin! I vin!' And he was going crazy. And then, we were like, 'Okay, so who's going to tell him?' When we did tell him, he slammed it down. He said something in Croatian that you could never repeat in English."

Drago reveled in turning the tables. Albert was a freshly minted lawyer and had bought a new car, and he went out to celebrate his newfound success one night with Tommy and a few friends. Somehow, at two in the morning, Albert's car had a personal encounter with one hundred feet of chain-link fence at a friendly neighborhood cemetery.

"Drago hears the story," Albert said, "and the next time I see him, he says, 'So, you don't need funeral home. You go straight to graveyard!'"

Throughout their fifty-nine-year love story, Drago and Klara were a complementary vision of unity. They had far different personalities, but it always worked.

With Uncle Drago, nephew A. J. Lulich said, "There was always a line in the sand that you knew not to cross, but you could always push the line. With Teta Klara, you didn't even want to walk in the sand. You could play with Drago, but you didn't play with Teta Klara or you'd be playing with fire. Klara was his sugar, and he was very protective of her. That's a strong woman right there."

Drago and Klara cut the cake at their surprise twenty-fifth wedding anniversary party in 1983. Longtime waitress Brittney Montes de Oca, who used her earnings at Drago's to pay for nursing school and later cared for Drago at the end of his life, said Klara and Drago's relationship was "a love story."

In 1995, just before Mardi Gras, Tommy and Gerry pulled off one of their best ruses. Drago was seventy-two, and he and his family attended the coronation ball for the Krewe of Argus. Drago went as a courtesy to his good friend, Jean-Luc Albin of Maurice's Bakery, because he thought Albin would be announced as king.

The normal procedure at the ball was for the krewe's captains—usually Bob DeViney and Ron Passons—to go from table to table with a crown and playfully place it on the head of the prospective king.

Usually, the only person besides DeViney and Passons who knew the identity of the new king was the king himself.

As DeViney and Passons kept placing the crown on different heads, the trumpets would sound, "Dah-Dahm!" But, as Shakespeare once wrote, uneasy lies the head that wears the crown.

"After trying four or five guys who said they weren't the king, they turned around and said, 'Okay, let's try this guy,' and they put the crown on Drago's head," Tommy said. "He said, 'Oh no, it ain't me,' and they said, 'Yeah, it is!' Usually, nobody in the room knows who the king's going to be other than the king and the captains. In our case, almost everybody knew who the king was going to be except for Drago."

When Tommy and Gerry came over to pledge their allegiance to the king, he was overcome with emotion.

"We just kind of stood him up—he had a tuxedo on—and put the sash and medallion on him," Tommy said. "Lo and behold, he realized we had sandbagged him."

In mythology, Argus had one hundred eyes that never closed, and now Drago was trying to recapture in his mind's eye his personal journey, which included terror, war, fear, uncertainty, and hunger.

And now he was King Argus XI, reigning over a parade with the theme, "Argus Celebrates the Great American Holidays."

Thanksgiving came nine months early that year.

"It can only happen in America," said Klara, who met her husband at Mardi Gras in 1958. "If it wouldn't have been for Carnival, there would not be our sons, Tommy and Gerry. Can you imagine how Drago and I felt when Tommy and Gerry actually surprised Drago? It was the first time anyone from Croatia had been king. A lot of people in the United States—or anywhere else—will not understand the meaning of being king of a parade on Mardi Gras day. He was amazed because he loved Mardi Gras. He always loved Mardi Gras."

The royal family lineage continued in the next few years. In 1998, Gerry was named King Argus XIV, and Tommy reigned as King Argus XXI in 2005, the last Mardi Gras before Hurricane Katrina. Cousin Johnny Matesich was King Argus XXXI in 2015, when Tommy's eldest daughter Maddie reigned as queen. Maddie's younger sister Callie was queen in 2021.

In 1995, Gerry and Tommy used a bit of subterfuge to give Drago the surprise of his life: he would reign as King Argus XI on Mardi Gras.

The weather for King Drago on Mardi Gras day in 1995 was bleak—the metropolitan area was pounded with nearly an inch of rain—but his royal highness was all smiles when Mike Hoss of WWL-TV climbed a ladder to interview him as the king's float stopped at the reviewing stand.

"Nice to see you, Mike," King Drago said, raising his scepter to the crowd. "It's not raining up here. . . . The weather's not too bad. It's a beautiful day, beautiful sunshine! Look at those people who are happy. Who cares about raining! We are enjoying Mardi Gras! We are having fun! Everybody loves New Orleans! Everybody loves Mardi Gras!"

Family friend Eddie Esposito, who waited tables at Drago's and later became a restaurant business consultant, said he recalled Drago practicing his scepter wave for a month in preparation for the ride.

"When he was still doing it a few weeks after the parade was

In 1998, with Drago at his side, Gerry reigned as King Argus XIV.

over, Klara had to remind him that his king days were over, and he had to can the wave," Esposito said, laughing.

Vera Buconic Occhipinti, Klara's younger cousin who came to New Orleans in the early 1960s to care for Tommy and Gerry, remembers Drago sitting in his chair near the bar, reviewing the parade of customers and giving them a wave and a smile. Long after the parade had passed, he was still King Drago.

"He would sit there and watch, and everybody would come talk to him," Vera said. "And he talked to anyone who came in."

One of Drago's greatest thrills in the final ten to fifteen years of his life—after his shucking days had come to an end—was to clean and bleach oyster shells and then paint them for special occasions such as birthdays or anniversaries or just to say "Welcome!" They became keepsakes, almost like a Muses shoe or a Zulu coconut, and he passed out thousands to customers.

"He wasn't as far along as Zulu, but he was ahead of Muses with his painted and decorated oyster shells," Tommy said. "He was the pioneer in painting oyster shells. Now it's second nature to have art on oyster shells."

In 2007, one of José Rodriguez's duties at the restaurant—actually, he considered it a perk—was to drive to Drago's house at around two in the afternoon, in between lunch and dinner shifts, and transport the patriarch to the restaurant he had built. José was an "expediter," somewhat like the quarterback in the kitchen who makes sure the plates roll out on time.

"It was really just a five- or ten-minute ride in Metairie," José said, "but he took me all around the world in that car. We talked about Croatia and fishing. I felt like I was in Europe, but I was in Metairie. He told me stories about him fishing and doing the oysters, just being a humble man. It was obviously important for him and Miss Klara and Tommy to leave a legacy for the family, and it's an honor to be a part of that legacy."

José had an earlier connection with Drago. When his father, Frank Rodriguez, proposed to his mother, Florisa, in 1971, he popped the

Drago was inspired by his life on the Adriatic Sea. He would reminisce about his fishing days with Drago's kitchen expediter José Rodriguez.

question at Drago's just-opened restaurant in Metairie.

"My dad was so nervous about proposing that he forgot his wallet, and he had to tell the waiter when the bill came," José said. "So, my dad told Mr. Drago, 'I asked her to marry me. Let me go back to my house, get my wallet, and come back.' And Mr. Drago said, 'Did she say yes?' And my dad said, 'Yes.' So Mr. Drago said, 'Let's celebrate at the bar with a glass of champagne!' Mr. Drago said, 'The meal's on me.'"

Drago also had a fatherly knack for knowing exactly what to say when his kids needed it the most. When Gerry, then twenty-seven, was in his medical school residency and had broken up with his girlfriend, he fell into a deep funk over the end of their relationship.

"In his broken English, my dad asked me, 'Why are you so upset? Did you think you were going to marry her?'" Gerry recalled.

Gerry was in no mood to hear it.

"Just shut up," he told his dad.

"You want to find your wife?" Drago continued. "Come with me. We're going to St. Clement of Rome, and I'll show you the eighth graders."

"And I'll be damned, he was right," Gerry said. "At the time, the eighth graders would have been fourteen, and I was twenty-seven, and there's thirteen years difference between me and my wife Heidi."

Heidi was not an eighth grader at St. Clement of Rome, but she did fit the criteria Drago laid down for his son in seeking a soulmate. When Gerry took Drago on a trip to the World Cup in France in 1998, he told his father he was thinking of proposing to Heidi.

"He told me, 'You know, when you get married, you look for the mother of your children. She looks like she will be good mother,'" Gerry recalled. "That was such smart, smart advice."

Heidi was so taken with Drago's warmth and love that she asked him to walk her down the aisle at her wedding in 1999 as her dad had already passed away. Drago was proud to do so, and he even accompanied Gerry and Heidi on their honeymoon to Europe.

Near the end of his life, when Drago was admitted to East Jefferson General Hospital, Brittney Montes de Oca, who had paid her way through nursing school by waiting tables at Drago's, was assigned by her nursing supervisor to care for him.

At Gerry's 1999 wedding in Key West, Florida, Drago walked Gerry's bride Heidi down the aisle. Heidi's father had passed away a short time before the wedding.

"Everybody on my floor knew I had worked at Drago's, and it was comforting to have someone he knew to take care of him," Brittney said. "It was hard, but I'm glad I was there. The night before he went home to hospice, the whole family was there, and Drago sang for us. He died later that week."

Brittney said her life was enriched by watching the love story between Drago and Klara unfold before her eyes.

"You could tell they were a love story," Brittney said. "Drago didn't go anywhere without this little hat that he had. It kind of snaps in the front. Miss Klara would always straighten his hat for him. He loved her, and she loved him. I always used to say, 'I want to be them when I grow up.'"

17

The Shirt

Drago could take a joke. That's why everyone loved him.

One Sunday afternoon, Drago and Klara threw a pool party for the kids and their friends, and somehow—no one remembers exactly if there was a friendly push or a daredevil move involved—Tommy and Gerry's first cousin A. J. Lulich wound up cannonballing into the water with all of his clothes on.

When A. J. jumped out of the pool soaking wet, he had nothing dry to slip on. Since he and Gerry had made plans to catch dinner and drinks at a restaurant on the West End that evening, Gerry led A. J. into Drago's bedroom and began rummaging through the closet to find something for his cousin to wear.

There, resting proudly on a hanger, was an exclusive, dry-clean-only shirt made by the haute couture London haberdasher, Hardy Amies, that Klara had bought Drago years earlier as a nod to his love of tennis.

There was only one problem with the shirt: It was alternately described as hideous, obnoxious, or ghastly. It was bright yellow with multiple green tennis courts splattered in a multi-directional pattern, one part psychedelic and one part Rorschach test.

"I remember thinking to myself, 'Let me just give A. J. something that Drago doesn't wear,' because when you loan something out of your closet to somebody, odds are you're not getting it back," Gerry recalled, laughing. "I remember going into the closet, and my mom had gone to one of the best men's stores in the town, and she bought him this expensive designer shirt. My mom paid ridiculous money for it, and Drago didn't like it, so he never ever wore it, as a matter of fact. It was a stupid shirt with tennis courts on it. So, I said, 'I'll give this to A. J.' That was the easiest thing to do."

When Drago saw A. J. in his shirt for the first time, Tommy said he gave him the full inquisition.

"A. J. said, 'Drago, my shirt's wet because I got thrown in the pool, but I'm going home, and I'll bring it back to you,'" Tommy recalled. "After that, Drago would always ask A. J., 'Where is my shirt? Where is my shirt?' He was just chomping at A. J. all the time, looking for the shirt. So then, another event goes by, and, all of a sudden, somebody else walks up, and they've got the shirt on. And Drago says, 'Hey, hey, hey, that is my shirt! That is my shirt!' Drago never got his shirt back. This became the 'tennis court' shirt, and after that, it would only come out for special and rare occasions."

The universe of shirt-wearers expanded as A. J., and then other friends and family and even total strangers would borrow it for occasions, big and small, to tease Drago into faux apoplexy.

"It was like the ugliest shirt in the whole freakin' closet," A. J. said. "It was a shirt Drago never wore, but after I started wearing it, it became like, 'Hey, you took my shirt! You took my shirt!' So, I would bring the shirt back after I wore it. He would clean it, and as soon as it was clean, I'd take it again just to fire him up. I'd go to the restaurant with his shirt on, and Drago would be, 'Klara, Klara, it's no fair! He's wearing my shirt!' He never even liked the shirt before, but then all of a sudden, with me wearing it, it was his favorite shirt."

A. J. and his friend Eddie Esposito spent so much time on weekends sleeping at Drago and Klara's house that they had plenty of opportunities to "borrow" the shirt and elevate Drago's temperature.

"Eddie and I were like the house guests that wouldn't go away," A. J. said. "We were like the sons he never wanted."

Gerry said the shirt was on its way to becoming a cherished piece of family lore.

"Drago always loved to hate A. J., and he was like, 'That's my shirt, give me my shirt!' and we all laughed and teased him," Gerry said. "From that point on, that shirt somehow wound up resurfacing every six months. Somebody else would wear it. It would always be a way to tease him."

Sometimes, Drago even joined in the fun. When Esposito was

getting married and held his bachelor's party at the restaurant, his friend, attorney Albert Nicaud, built a wooden cake on wheels that could be rolled out for the traditional pop-out dance.

"The top was round, and I went into the kitchen and got some freezer paper and put it on the top," Albert said. "Well, Drago got inside the cake, and we rolled out the cake and started playing the 'nah-nah-nah' music. Then, Drago pops out of the cake holding a tennis racket and wearing this disgusting shirt."

When Gerry graduated from medical school, one of his friends showed up wearing the shirt. At one point, Tommy decided to place the shirt in a frame.

"After that, the shirt would come out for certain events like birthday parties or somebody would come put it on on Christmas afternoon—and every time, Drago would shout, 'Hey, that is my shirt!'" Tommy said.

Drago's infamous yellow-and-green tennis shirt—which popped up in the craziest places to Drago's feigned anger and amusement—would make a command appearance at major events.

There was even an interregnum when the shirt disappeared and then resurfaced, like a bad penny, a few years later in Tommy's house.

At Drago's funeral in 2017, Tommy ended the eulogy he delivered on behalf of his father by pulling out "the Shirt" and holding it up to the congregation of mourners at St. Clement of Rome Church in Metairie.

"Drago, don't worry about it," Tommy said. "I've got your shirt. I'm going to hold it for you."

18
Baby Steps

On October 1, 1991, Klara was on the phone with her youngest sister Mira in Dubrovnik.

"They are coming here!" Mira told Klara. "I saw the enemy planes in the air, and they bombed the fort on top of the mountain . . ."

At that moment, the phone went dead.

The alarm in Mira's voice—she had told Klara that the family house was burning and that their mother Marija had had a heart attack—understandably sent Klara into a tizzy. She knew that the Croatian forces defending the historic city of Dubrovnik from the Serbian backed Yugoslav People's Army (JNA) were now officially under attack.

For the next several hours, from her travel agency office in Metairie, Klara and two associates, Evie Schellang and Mary Ann Hawkins, kept calling Mira's number, trying to reestablish a connection.

"I was having a heart attack," Klara said. "I didn't know anything about what was happening or how my mother and sisters and their families were. I saw the Hotel Imperial in Dubrovnik on fire on the television, and our family home is 200 yards away from there. All three of us stayed on the phone until eleven o'clock that night until finally one of us got through."

When Klara was able to talk again to her shaken sister, she got a relatively good update from Mira. Their house did not catch on fire. A cluster bomb had landed a few yards from the side of the house, setting plants ablaze and filling the house with smoke.

"It turned out my mom had just passed out," Klara said. "She fainted because she was in the kitchen probably close to where the bomb fell, but she was protected by a sturdy wall."

Two and a half months before war officially broke out, Klara wrote a letter to the editor of the *Times-Picayune* in which she laid out her perspective on the gathering storm. Earlier in July, the Serbian-backed army had begun its attacks outside Dubrovnik after Croatia and neighboring Slovenia had declared their independence.

"I am a Croat," Klara wrote. "I was born and lived in Dubrovnik, where I spent the first eighteen years of my life. I am not against Serbs. I have many dear friends who are Serbs. My brother-in-law was a Serb. My home in New Orleans was always open to Serbs. LSU had two Serbs among their basketball players for a few years, and my home was their home away from home. I am against those Serbs who are ruling Yugoslavia today and control the army and are responsible for the attack on Slovenes and Croats this past month [July]. What is happening today in Yugoslavia is not civil war. It is aggression of the Serbian Communist army on innocent people."

For three months, Dubrovnik was under heavy siege, without access to electrical power or running water. Klara's sister said the family saved their urine to flush the toilet.

Klara sprang into action, organizing an ad hoc group of friends and Croatian Americans—Louisiana Citizens for a Free Croatia—that collected hundreds of thousands of dollars' worth of food, clothing and medical supplies for her homeland. Drago's Restaurant initially became the unofficial headquarters for the local Croatian relief effort.

Klara and Eddie Esposito, a Drago's waiter, flew to Munich, Germany, and then drove to Klagenfurt, Austria, to rendezvous with Croatians who could take the supplies into territories they controlled. On a parallel track, Klara's grassroots organization urged the U.S. to recognize Croatia as a sovereign state.

Klara found out in the weeks after the October 1 attack that her sister had been shot at by a sniper and her mother was handing out clothes to a desperate woman who had come to her door.

The Croatian relief supplies that originally came into Drago's Restaurant had to be stored in the bar area, and Drago's had to turn down a party rental at the bar because of the tight squeeze.

"In the end, people will respect us for this," Klara's son Gerry said.

The relief effort soon shifted to a non-profit umbrella group Klara organized known as Feed My Sheep, whose board included retired New Orleans Archbishop Philip Hannan, a WWII paratrooper chaplain with the Eighty-second Airborne Division, as well as other local businessmen and several veteran Catholic pilgrims who had visited Medjugorje, Croatia.

Even though she had lived in New Orleans for thirty years, Klara only met Archbishop Hannan for the first time in 1991 when she became the public voice in New Orleans for Croatian relief. As a staunch anti-communist, Archbishop Hannan interviewed Klara every Wednesday night on his FOCUS television show, which covered Catholic response to world events.

"I was on to give reports on what was happening in Yugoslavia, and it did help promote the cause," Klara said. "Everyone knew from that program that Croatia was trying to break from Communism. I traveled three times to Europe with Archbishop Hannan because the archbishop wanted to tell the people of America what was going on. It was all aimed at educating the people."

Klara also traveled with Archbishop Hannan to Rome in 2000 for the canonization of St. Katharine Drexel, the Philadelphia heiress who founded the Sisters of the Blessed Sacrament and went on to establish schools and churches for African Americans and Native Americans across the United States. Among the schools St. Katharine founded was Xavier University of Louisiana, which annually places more African Americans in medical school than any other college in the United States.

Well into his nineties, Archbishop Hannan made a point of downing as many charbroiled oysters as he could.

Archbishop Hannan also was keenly interested in Klara's connections to Medjugorje. It was in Medjugorje—about twenty-three miles from Klara's birthplace of Stupa—where in 1981 six local children reported seeing visions of the Blessed Virgin Mary.

Medjugorje played an important role in Klara's spiritual and professional life. As word spread across the globe about what was occurring in the village, thousands flocked there to see for themselves, and, as a travel agent, Klara booked dozens of pilgrimages there for New Orleans Catholics in the 1980s and 1990s. She herself

Klara and Drago joined New Orleans Archbishop Philip Hannan at the 2000 canonization of St. Katharine Drexel in Rome. St. Katharine founded Xavier University of Louisiana in 1925.

made twenty trips to the site where the faithful said the apparitions occurred. She visited churches across south Louisiana to relate her experiences and even translated for the visionaries when they made church talks in the Archdiocese of New Orleans.

While Pope Francis approved Catholic pilgrimages to Medjugorje in May 2019, he stopped short of making a declaration on the authenticity of the apparitions. Catholics are not bound to believe in the apparitions, but Klara can't explain some of the things she has witnessed, particularly the spiritual transformations she has observed in people who have visited.

"I have seen it, and I do believe," Klara said. "People who have made pilgrimages to Medjugorje have seen some miraculous things, but even those who have not experienced those things have come back converted. The experience of being in Medjugorje and praying to the Blessed Mother has changed their lives. Yes, Medjugorje has grown to become more commercial as a tourist attraction these days, but I can't lose sight of the reality of how many people's lives have been transformed to the good."

Klara's sister Nada's late husband, who grew up as a member of the Communist party, had one such experience. He and Nada were driving on the highway near Medjugorje one day when all of a sudden they heard a ringing sound coming from their car's engine. It lasted for ninety minutes.

"It was ringing like a bell," Klara said. "He stopped at a service station, and the ringing wouldn't stop. They continued driving and it wouldn't stop. Then Nada saw the sign for Medjugorje, and she said, 'Turn in.' He turned in, and the bell stopped ringing. So he brought her close to the church and told her, 'Take whatever time you need.' After she got back, he didn't know what to say. They drove the car back to Dubrovnik, and there was no more bell, even though it had been ringing for an hour and a half. He became a believer. He had been baptized Eastern Orthodox. We saw him just before he died of carcinoma, and he was calling for God."

Klara's church visits in connection with the apparitions at Medjugorje had raised her public profile throughout south Louisiana, giving her a strong platform to advocate for relief for the Croatian people when war erupted in 1991.

One of her initial thoughts was to help bring Croatian children to the U.S., at least temporarily, to keep them safe or to find adoptive families, but Croatian authorities told her they did not want their children adopted by foreigners.

Most of the relief shipments Klara organized were transported in large shipping containers. Each load could hold up to 40,000 pounds of lentils, flour, or rice, baby milk and cereal, medical equipment, and clothing. Her Croats also needed rebuilding materials. When the space to drop off supplies at Drago's became too tight, Hubie and Kay Mule offered their religious and office supply store in Metairie as a staging area. The Mules became staunch supporters of the local Croatian relief effort.

"Croatia needed hammers and nails so they could return the people to their homes and start their farms again," Klara said. "I made a pledge to help the people. As long as I could and had the strength, I wanted to help. I also did it for Archbishop Hannan, because he helped the Croatian cause so much. I thought, 'What could I do for a man who had everything?' and this was it."

In December 1991, among Klara's most pressing concerns was the wellbeing of her newly born great niece, Deša, the daughter of her niece, Sandi Tesanovic. Deša was just six months old when Klara and Drago worked back channels to get both Sandi and her baby out of Croatia.

"They had sent all the women and children north, close to the Italian border," Klara said. "I said, 'I'm going to get that girl over here.' I didn't want her to be in a refugee camp, which was like a prison camp."

Klara thought for a moment. Her first call was to Archbishop Hannan, who as a priest chaplain in WWII, had the wherewithal to protect the treasures of the cathedral in 1945 in Cologne, Germany.

"I told the archbishop I needed help—that I needed to get to some very influential people in Munich or Frankfurt—to help get my niece and her baby out of Yugoslavia," Klara said. "The archbishop sent some papers to the archbishop of Munich, and we had no problem getting visas for them. Sandi came on the train from Yugoslavia, and we met her at the train station."

Sandi, who was twenty-seven at the time, wrestled with the decision to leave her husband behind with the war raging, but Deša already had come down with pneumonia, and there was no running water or electricity in Dubrovnik.

"My husband told me, 'Go save the baby and be happy,'" Sandi said.

Sandi and Deša arrived by train in Munich around Christmastime.

"I will never forget when I was walking out of the train and looking to my right, and nobody was there," Sandi said. "Then I turned my head to the left, and I saw Teta Klara running to hug me. It meant the whole world to me. You can't imagine a situation without water, without electricity, with bombs going off and no food, no diapers, no hope. We were surrounded by the enemy."

On a previous trip to New Orleans before the outbreak of the war, Sandi had begun referring to Drago as "Daddy."

Sandi's father had died in 1988, and Drago made sure when she left New Orleans to return to Croatia that she knew he would always be there to protect her: "Daddy told me, 'Baby, whatever you need, you just call me. If you have no money, call me 'collect' and I will send you whatever you want. I know you love tuna fish, and I will send you as much tuna fish as you want. Your father will always be a father for you, but now I am here, and I will do for you whatever you need.'"

When Sandi and Deša finally arrived safely in New Orleans, Drago took Sandi to the grocery store.

"Daddy told me to take the carriage, and he filled it with bread and with diapers," Sandi recalled. "I tried to tell him, 'No, Daddy, diapers are expensive,' but he kept filling the carriage with fruit, cakes, waffles, and marmalade."

Sandi and Deša remained in New Orleans for six months, enjoying the hot tub at Klara and Drago's house, singing on the phone to her relatives back home and "dancing on the nice blue floor of Teta Klara's bedroom."

"They were full of love," Sandi said.

Then, two months later, when Deša was just eight months old, she took her first steps on the bar at Drago's.

Deša, now in her early thirties, is a physician in Dubrovnik, just like her mother and father.

"Of course, I have no memories of walking on the bar, but whenever I do come back to the restaurant, I can remember the distinct smell," Deša said. "It's the same smell that I can remember from my earliest childhood when I came to New Orleans for the summers. I get this feeling of security from all the people when I am there—from Tommy, Gerry, Teta Klara, and Drago, when he was alive. It's the smells and the warmth of everything around me."

In December 1992, with the shelling largely limited to areas outside of Dubrovnik, Klara made her first visit back home since the war began. She marveled that the Marian shrine in Medjugorje had been untouched by the bombing.

"It makes you wonder if this is one of the miracles of Medjugorje or if the Serbians were just afraid to attack it," Klara said.

Her birthplace home in Stupa was hit by fifty-five grenades, and her uncle was still living in a part of the house that still had a roof. All

Deša Tesanovic, the daughter of Klara's niece Sandi, was just eight months old when she took her first steps on the bar at Drago's. Klara and Drago worked back channels to get both Sandi and little Deša out of Croatia at the outset of the 1991 war.

seventy of the villagers were dressed in black because they were in mourning—six men from the village had been killed, and more than forty villages between Dubrovnik and Stupa had been destroyed.

In a little more than a year, Klara's Feed My Sheep nonprofit organization managed to ship fifteen to twenty containers of supplies to Croatia. She even stared down officials on the dock in Dubrovnik when they said a container filled with $5,000 worth of children's shoes, destined for a Dubrovnik orphanage, could not be found.

"I probably was a little bit ugly and rude, but the container arrived the next day," she said.

In 1993, Klara and Drago opened their home in Metairie to war victims, including Serbs. One of the injured, Edin Donlic, had been flown to the U.S. for facial surgery after being hit by shrapnel. He needed multiple facial reconstruction surgeries.

"His jaw was wired shut because he had a broken jaw," Klara said. "Doctors gave him pliers for the flight in case he felt he had to throw up on the plane and needed to have his mouth open."

Drago shows off a traditional Croatian costume at a friendly bocce ball competition in 1982. Klara was thrilled to play a part in Croatia's independence a decade later.

Another young man, a Muslim named Ennis, needed multiple urologic surgeries due to pelvic injuries.

One night, at the former Par 4's bar on Canal Boulevard, Tommy, Gerry, Edin, and Ennis were joined by Gerry's old roommate, Nebojsa, a Serb, and WWL sportscaster Mike Hoss.

"Mike couldn't stop talking about how while a war was raging over there, we had Serbs, Croats, and Muslims drinking together in New Orleans," Gerry said.

Klara's staggering relief efforts were recognized by Croatia in 1995 with its highest civilian award—the Red Danice Hrvatske—which was presented by President Franjo Tudjman, who led Croatia to independence from Yugoslavia in 1991. The Dayton Peace Agreement, signed in Paris in December 1995, formally ended the three-and-a-half-year war.

As vice president of the National Federation of Croatian Americans, Klara also participated in high-level meetings at the White House in December 1995 with First Lady Hillary Clinton to discuss the Dayton Peace Agreement. In January 1996, she returned to the White House for a reception to highlight humanitarian assistance to the people of the region. The personal invitation to attend the White House meetings came directly from Mrs. Clinton.

"She mentioned that the meeting would be to discuss how Serbian women had been abused by Croatian soldiers," Klara said. "I told her I would be glad to come as a representative, but we also needed to talk about how Croatian women had been abused by the Serbians."

Klara also received the national Leadership Award from the National Federation of Croatian Americans (NFCA) "for outstanding achievement in business and civic affairs."

"When the war broke out, that took my patriotism and activism to another level," said Steve Rukavina, the long-time president of the NFCA, who enjoyed working with Klara to advocate for Croatian-American issues.

Klara said her activism on behalf of her homeland was in part a gift she wanted to give to her husband.

"That was his lifetime dream—for Croatia to become Croatia," Klara said. "Croatia was a kingdom in the 900s, and Drago always had Croatia in his heart and in his soul. Drago allowed me to help

Klara participated in high-level meetings at the White House in December 1995 with First Lady Hillary Clinton to discuss the Dayton Peace Agreement that ended the Croatian War.

with the formation of Croatia. I did it for my family, for my country, and for my husband."

In February 1996, Klara returned to Croatia for the national celebration of the Feast of St. Blaise, the patron saint of Dubrovnik. For decades, the Communist government had not permitted any large, formal celebrations on the saint's feast day, February 3, and only "a few brave ones" took to the streets of Old Town Dubrovnik to participate in the traditional procession.

What Klara saw in 1996 overwhelmed her: The exterior of the church of St. Blaise was covered with thousands of lights. Exquisite wreaths and fragrant garlands of bay leaves bedecked the city, and white flags bearing the image of St. Blaise and the word *"Libertas"* were waved by freedom lovers through the streets.

"I left Yugoslavia to find in my new country, America, all the rights that had been denied to me there," Klara said. "For the first time in many people's lives, they could freely worship God. They had freedom of speech and of the press."

In 2022, Klara received the Pope John Paul II Award from the Catholic Community Foundation for her lifetime of service and philanthropy. St. John Paul II, who was ordained as an underground priest in Poland and later became one of the most important figures in the fall of the Iron Curtain, is one of Klara's heroes.

Two of the most memorable moments of her life came when she was invited to greet the first Slavic pope in 1994 upon his arrival at the Zagreb airport. It was the first visit by a pope to Croatia since its people had become Roman Catholics more than one thousand years earlier. She also was invited to Baltimore in 1995 to bid farewell to the pope at the conclusion of his visit to the U.S.

"I've received so many awards, and they all are well received, but this one was super special," Klara said. "He was my favorite pope, the pope who fought Communism. This is what my father was involved in. This is what motivated me. I always watched him and said, 'Hurray for him!' He was a Polish friend."

If Klara ever needed motivation to persevere in her humanitarian work, all she had to do was recall the day her great niece Deša took her first steps atop the bar at Drago's—thousands of miles away from the bombs and the bullets in Dubrovnik.

For Klara, the price of Croatian freedom was worth every baby step.

19

Katrina: "A Moral Obligation"

Like most New Orleanians in August 2005, Klara and Drago Cvitanovich and their sons Tommy and Gerry figured they would accept the slow crawl out of the city in advance of Hurricane Katrina as a small price to pay for living in one of America's most fascinating cities—and then be back in their homes and returning to work by the end of the following week.

Tommy wasn't even considering evacuating on the Saturday before Katrina. In fact, he was on the last flight *into* New Orleans on Saturday night, August 27, after having attended a birthday party in New York in honor of his first cousin, David Cvitanovich Jr.

The celebration had to be cut short because of the ominous weather warnings.

"I was there on the birthday trip for Dave with about ten other Croatian fishermen," Tommy recalled. "We were in Yankee Stadium watching the Yankees play the Kansas City Royals. They had just developed these radar apps for the phone, and the guys were looking at their phones and saying, 'Look at this!' The game ended around 4:30 p.m., and we caught the last Jet Blue flight back into New Orleans. We landed on Saturday at midnight."

As the radar blew up late Saturday night and into Sunday morning, August 28, Tommy felt, mostly because of his parents and kids, it was wise to play it safe. Gerry already had decided to make the seventeen-hour drive to Houston with his wife and their children.

"On Sunday afternoon, Tommy said, 'Let's go!'" Klara recalled. "We left from here not knowing where we were going to go. It took us fourteen hours to get to Baton Rouge. We were behind a bus where an elderly person had just died, and the traffic wasn't moving. We finally got to Baton Rouge, and Tommy had a friend who was a manager of the Hampton Inn, and he told Tommy, 'I have one room.' So, all of us squeezed into one room with two double beds, just like my family did in Dubrovnik during the war."

Longtime kitchen manager Freddie McKnight, who lived in Metairie, found out on Sunday that Tommy was evacuating. Freddie asked if he and some family members could ride out the storm at the restaurant, which has three floors, and Tommy quickly agreed.

Freddie and several relatives sheltered on the second floor. They were joined the next day by Preston Whitfield, a chef who lived in Metairie and who woke up on Tuesday, August 30, to knee deep water in his apartment and waded from his flooded neighborhood to Drago's, which was, for the most part, high and dry except when passing cars created waves.

The restaurant, with its freezers and refrigerators stocked with food for a busy weekend, had lost electrical power. At first, Freddie and Preston cooked primarily for themselves and their family members, using a propane grill.

"We were grilling steaks, frying shrimp, grilling chicken—whatever was in the restaurant," Freddie said.

It took about three or four days for Tommy to get back into the city from Baton Rouge. After securing plane tickets to Texas for Freddie's two children so that they could be reunited with their mother, Tommy came back to Metairie and slept on the second floor with his kitchen crew. Tommy's house, just a ten-minute drive from the restaurant in Fat City, had lost its roof and was in shambles.

The restaurant was in far better shape. Although there was no power, a portable generator kicked in to run a TV and a few fans, mostly recirculating the hot air. And, as long as the doors to the coolers and freezers remained closed except for quick in-and-outs, the food could last for a relatively long time.

"Some of us had air mattresses, and I think Tommy brought some air mattresses, too," Freddie said. "A couple of times I slept outside on the balcony because it was super hot. We could watch TV, but it was showing the same things about the disaster, over and over and over. It would drive you crazy."

Freddie said initially he started cooking in the back lot behind the restaurant.

"We had to eat, so we tried to use as much stuff out of the cooler first before it would go bad," Freddie said. "Then we went into the freezer. We were cooking chicken and hamburgers, and we had a full bar. We had all the food and drink you could ever need to eat or drink."

The smells that began wafting from their outdoor cookouts served as smoke signals to passersby.

"We were just cooking this stuff, and we knew it would go bad, so if anybody wanted it, we would let them have it," Freddie said. "We were feeding people out of the back door for the first couple of days before Tommy came in for good. When people would pass at breakfast or lunch time, they would ask, 'You got anything extra?' and we would give it to them. When Tommy found out we were doing that, he decided that since people were coming back in to check on their houses, he would move everything out to the front. When Tommy moved it out front, that definitely helped get the word out."

On Monday, September 5—just a week after Katrina—Drago's served 500 meals in the parking lot: 250 to the Coast Guard and 250 to others. The next day's total was 1,300 meals of pasta, chicken, and sausage to first responders, relief workers and returning neighbors, and that increased to anywhere from 1,800 to 3,400 meals a day.

"The reason we know how many people we served was that we were buying plastic containers, and we could keep a count of how many meals we served," Klara said. "As soon as people found out there was hot food and could smell it, they were coming in droves. We were no longer just cooking for the people plugging the levees. It was for everybody."

Tommy said it was the least he could do considering his restaurant had survived relatively unscathed.

"My mom and I said, 'We've got good food left over, and it's still good, it's still cold,'" Tommy said. "It was the right thing to do."

He also was motivated by the generational example of Ruth Fertel, the founder and owner of Ruth's Chris Steak House in New Orleans, who fed her Mid-City neighbors after Hurricane Betsy devastated the city in 1965.

"My mom was worried about me going into New Orleans, but I reminded her about the inspiration that Ruth Fertel had provided after Betsy, when she helped feed people who had hurricane damage," Tommy said. "Everyone remembered Ruth's efforts, and I said I wanted people to remember that Drago's was there helping after Hurricane Katrina. It was scary because there really was no place for people who were there to get food. We were it. That picture of hundreds of people standing in line to eat made an impression. I sure never expected to see a Depression-like soup line in this country."

A couple of TV stations did reports on the impromptu meal service, and every day, more people began arriving at the Drago's parking lot, in cars and on foot.

"We would go from 10:30 a.m. or 11:00 a.m. until we'd run out; about two o'clock," Tommy said.

The only things Drago's did not serve in that initial wave were

An aerial view of the post-Katrina food line extending outside of the Drago's parking lot.

oysters. Tommy had 140 sacks stored in a twenty-by-forty-foot seafood cooler, but the loss of electricity meant they had to be thrown out.

"We left that cooler closed as long as we could because we were waiting for the insurance adjusters," Tommy recalled. "When we finally opened it and loaded everything into a trailer, I was thinking to myself, 'God help the people who are driving behind this trailer when it's going across the Huey P. Long Bridge!' It stunk. To this day, that might be the worst odor ever."

Drago's massive and well-insulated freezers were another story. Frozen food can stay cold for up to ten days or two weeks.

"We were throwing dry ice in there, which we brought in from Baton Rouge, to extend the life a little bit," Tommy said. "A freezer works like an ice chest because it's insulated. In the freezer we had sauces, proteins, and soups. We were mixing and matching left and right. We'd mix in a couple of cases of meatballs with red sauce and cook pasta. We also had two refrigerated trucks, so we transferred food from the freezer to the refrigerated trucks and kept that going for awhile."

Tommy said Drago's wasn't the only restaurant or food company responsible for the emergency food relief effort.

"We were the ones driving the train, but it was a freakin' long train," he said.

Blue Runner donated hundreds of cans of red beans. Uncle Ben's dropped off one hundred bags of rice, fifty pounds each. Drago's picked up commodities from food suppliers Sysco and Conco (now Reinhart) at their Elmwood facilities because the food suppliers could not deliver. Coca-Cola donated soft drinks by the pallet. There were donations from Kraft Foods, Kajun Kettle Foods, Whole Foods, Bill Goldring's Republic Beverage, and Greg Reggio's Zea's Rotisserie and Grill.

Perhaps the most intriguing donation came from Glenn Mistich, owner of the Gourmet Butcher Block, whose freezer in Metairie, cut off from power, was stocked with pallets of raw chicken and his famous turduckens, which otherwise would have been wasted.

Tommy was approached by Jefferson Parish officials who offered him a contract to provide emergency food services, but he decided in the end to continue with his all-volunteer effort.

"We didn't get a single penny from the government, or FEMA, or the parish, or the state," Tommy said. "It was all us and our friends. We were driving the train."

Drago's remained without grid power for three or four weeks but finally reopened for modified lunch business on Monday, September 26. In Jefferson Parish, more fast-food places and grocery stores were opening up, so the need was not as great as it was immediately after the storm.

Tommy and Klara then looked east and sensed it was time to shift their soup kitchen to New Orleans, where 80 percent of the city's homes had sustained flood damage because of the levee breaches.

The question was: where could Drago's set up shop to be most effective? Gerry said there was no question where the New Orleans operation would be staged.

"We decided to go back to our original neighborhood—Lakeview—where Gerry and I grew up," Tommy said. "I went to St. Dominic School for a year. St. Dominic is where we went to church as a family for decades. St. Dominic was a landmark in Lakeview."

"We knew that New Orleans was under siege," Klara added. "The other thing was, Drago knew most of the people in Lakeview. It was a good, central place that people could come to. We had a big sign on one of the trucks that said: 'FREE FOOD.'"

St. Dominic Church also is located in the same 700 block of Harrison Avenue as the original Drago's Seafood Restaurant, run by Drago's sister Gloria Cvitanovich Batinich, where Drago first worked after coming to New Orleans on his American visa in 1961.

"It was near a place where Drago had worked so long, so it meant a lot to me and Drago," Klara said. "That's where our kids basically grew up."

Klara attempted to contact the St. Dominic pastor to make sure he was okay with Drago's setting up its food service on the plaza in front of the church, but she couldn't get through to anyone.

She decided to try her good friend, former New Orleans Archbishop Philip Hannan, who was ninety-two and who had been retired since 1988. Just because he was retired didn't mean he couldn't grant Klara general absolution.

"I told Archbishop Hannan I was having trouble reaching anybody in the St. Dominic office to give us permission to serve the food in

The Cvitanovich family decided in October 2005 to set up a Drago's food truck in front of flooded St. Dominic Church in Lakeview to distribute free meals to returning residents. After Katrina, Drago's served 77,000 free meals in Metairie and New Orleans.

front of the church, and he said, 'Let *me* try,'" Klara said. "Two hours later, he called me back and said, 'I couldn't find anybody either. *I'm* giving you permission. If you get in trouble, I'm the one who's in trouble.' So, it was Archbishop Hannan who gave us permission."

"That's the classic example that you don't ask for permission, you ask for forgiveness later," Tommy said.

No one had to ask for forgiveness.

"I want to tell you, it was really cool being back at St. Dominic," Tommy said. "It was way different than in Metairie. I don't know exactly why that was. We didn't have a place in Metairie in the parking lot for people to sit down and have their meals, but at St. Dominic, there was this long, stone, sitting area, almost like a bench, that extended all around the front of the church where people could eat and talk. This was an incredible meeting place where neighbors and friends and their kids who went to St. Dominic or other schools

Free meals at St. Dominic started at noon daily until the daily ration ran out.

could sit and talk. The families in Lakeview were really embedded there. It seemed like everyone who received food knew each other."

They all asked each other the same question: "How many feet did you get?"

"It was a bond for everybody because everybody had the same story," Tommy said. "You either got six feet or ten feet, depending on if your house was above the ground or not."

Like so many adults with elderly parents during that stressful time, Tommy traces the worsening of his father's mental decline to Katrina.

"Katrina was right at the start of the downfall of my dad's mental capacity," he said. "That's when he got old. That's when he stopped driving. You could absolutely see it. He would sit in one of those folding chairs near the St. Dominic statue and people would come up to him and say, 'Hello, Mr. Drago. How ya doing? Good to see you.' My dad would say, 'Guut to see you! Guut to see you!'"

Klara said Drago never walked inside St. Dominic Church to view the damage, but Tommy did.

"The picture of what I remember most about Katrina was when I walked into St. Dominic Church and it looked like a flippin' bomb went off," Tommy said. "Pews were up on their sides, and there was mud everywhere. It literally looked like something blew up in there."

Klara was on the serving lines both in Metairie and New Orleans, probably touching three-quarters of the more than 77,000 meals Drago's handed out over two months. She also offered a listening ear, freeing people to release their pent-up emotions.

"A little old lady came up to speak to Drago, and she was crying," Klara said. "She said she had lost her husband a couple of years earlier, and he was a man who had taken care of everything for her. She thought she had insurance, but she didn't have flood insurance. She said, 'So, I don't have anything now. I don't have a husband, and I am lost.' Stories like that—horrible stories—move you, if you have a heart."

Gerry, meanwhile, had to focus on his medical work. His new urgent care clinic had just opened in Kenner, and water barely got into the lobby. While Drago's was giving away 77,000 free meals, Gerry's urgent care center was doing more than 5,000 free visits, most of them to administer tetanus shots for people returning home to clean out their homes.

The impact of Drago's post-Katrina feeding mission resonates to this day. Barely a day goes by when someone doesn't bring up to Klara or Tommy their thanks for what Drago's did by providing a hot meal in the post-Katrina chaos.

Mel Grodsky, manager of Porter Stevens men's clothing store in Lakeside, showed up several days in a row for food for his staff members.

"He kept wanting to pay my employees, but I said, 'We're not taking any money,'" Tommy said. "The next day, he brought us a painting of an alligator po'boy that had been hanging in his store, and he gave it to me. I said, 'Fine, I'll take it,' and I climbed up on a bar stool and hung it to a gas pipe near the ceiling with two wire ties, just inside the front door, and it's been there ever since. We've taken it down a couple of times to paint, but that's how it's always hung. Since then, some of our other restaurants have a similar piece of artwork."

The statue of St. Dominic in Lakeview still bears the water marks from the flooding from Hurricane Katrina. Drago's set up shop in front of their former church to provide free meals to families returning to piece together their lives.

When Tommy would not accept a dime from Porter Stevens' manager Mel Grodsky for providing free meals to his staff after Katrina, Grodsky gifted an alligator po'boy painting to the restaurant. It hangs just inside the front entrance.

Klara said when she walks in Lakeside or greets patrons at the restaurant or just bumps into people in the street, they still mention how much they cherished her gesture of kindness in their time of need.

"In this country, we were able to live the American dream to the fullest," Klara said. "Giving back makes us feel good, especially here in our own community. The people of New Orleans have been the key to our success. One thing it taught me is that it's much easier to be on the giving side than on the receiving side. I just felt that we had it and other people didn't, so we had to give it away. For me, it was a moral obligation and also my way of saying thank you to the city of New Orleans and the United States for all they had done for us."

20

Spreading the Love

Katrina was Armageddon for the New Orleans restaurant industry.

While Drago's reopened within a month after Katrina—Tommy set up ten FEMA trailers in the back lot for displaced workers—other restaurants never came back, some because they had been flooded and did not have enough insurance coverage, and others because they made a calculated business decision that a weakened New Orleans, on its knees, was not worth the heavy lifting.

Tommy's close affiliation with the Louisiana Restaurant Association and the National Restaurant Association made the defections from New Orleans by some restaurateurs even tougher to stomach.

Executives of Ruth's Chris Steak House, whose corporate offices were located directly behind their Metairie restaurant on Veterans Memorial Boulevard, decided to leave town. The exodus of the corporate office was a purely corporate decision, not one made by Tommy's friend, Lana Duke, the local genius and former advertising executive behind the marketing "sizzle" that helped put Ruth Fertel's steak empire on the national map.

"When they came here to look at the damage, within the next two or three days, they had made their decision that they were going to Orlando," Tommy said. "That was their executive team. The corporate office literally deserted us. They left the city. We even fed some people from Ruth's Chris who were packing up their headquarters to leave New Orleans. They were here picking up the computer servers and other vital equipment and moving away permanently."

Virtually every one of the approximately 3,400 restaurants in Orleans, Jefferson, and St. Bernard civil parishes closed in the immediate aftermath of Katrina, either as a result of direct damage from the storm or related power outages. Prior to Katrina, the restaurant industry comprised roughly 10 percent of the workforce in the metropolitan area, employing about 54,000 people.

One month after the storm, Tommy found himself playing the vital role of civic cheerleader.

"I think we are a strong and passionate people, and we won't be down for long," he assured one local reporter.

Tommy was drawing on his close relationships and years of experience as a board member of restaurant associations on the local, state, national, and even Canadian levels.

"I know what it's like to be a mom-and-pop and have a few hundred thousand dollars a year in sales," he said. "I know what it's like to struggle and to watch my mom and dad bust their tails and give up everything they had for this restaurant to survive. And, on the flip side, I know what it's like to run a $40 million operation and what it's like to run multiple units. I know the corporate side of it now. I have a certain perspective because I know both sides of the equation. I know what it's like to really struggle and make decisions. And I know what it's like to hire people who are smarter than you to help you make decisions. To me, one of the coolest things is when another restaurateur asks me for information and advice—someone who's struggling like my mom and dad struggled—and I have a good answer for them. To me, that's as satisfying as watching your son score a touchdown or your daughter do this great somersault as a cheerleader. That's how I feel when I'm around people like Emeril Lagasse or Ralph Brennan."

One of Tommy's biggest regrets is that he didn't have the opportunity to know Ruth Fertel at a deeper level before she died in 2002.

"I remember her coming into our restaurant a couple of times, but I wish I would have known her better," Tommy said. "Some of the things that I know she did, I do today. If I see something wrong, I'll go in the kitchen and I'll try to show the people how to do it right. If she went to one of her restaurants and the steak and mashed potatoes weren't exactly right, she'd say, 'Excuse me, guys.' And then she'd get up from her table and go into the kitchen and ask, 'Who's working that station?' and then tell them this and this and this. 'But don't make that mistake a second time.' The fact that she was so hands-on is something I take pride in doing myself. I know every position in our restaurant. Now, do I have people who can cook a lot faster than I can? Damn right, I do. But when people ask me certain questions, I know the answers."

Tommy, Drago, and Klara were so assured New Orleans could complete its comeback story that they decided to make one of the biggest gambles of their lives. In July 2007, with the New Orleans Saints back in town but with the city's future still not assured, they partnered with the New Orleans Hilton Riverside to open a second Drago's restaurant, seating 350 people, just off the hotel's main entrance.

"We're proud to be part of rebuilding New Orleans," Tommy declared.

In a nod to the philanthropy that Drago and Klara had always preached, the grand opening included a gala that raised $40,000 to benefit the New Orleans Police Department's Eighth District. The proceeds were earmarked for the purchase of special vehicles for the district, which serves the French Quarter, Central Business District, and the Warehouse District.

The occasion was even more festive because it also honored Drago on his eighty-fifth birthday. He sat in front of a giant cake topped, appropriately enough, by an oyster on the half shell. The day before this event, Little Drago was born to Gerry and Heidi.

In a matter of months, Drago's at the Hilton became the hotel chain's highest-grossing and most-profitable restaurant in the United States.

"My dad's name is on one of the busiest restaurants in the city of New Orleans," Tommy said. "That's pretty cool."

From that expansion, Tommy continued to seek out and pounce on new opportunities to spread charbroiled fever. He opened Drago's locations in Jackson, Mississippi (January 2015); in Lafayette (September 2017); in Baton Rouge (February 2019); in Lake Charles at the L'Auberge Casino Resort (September 2021); and in Bossier City (April 2023).

Drago's owns and operates its restaurants in Metairie, Lafayette, and Baton Rouge; the restaurants at the New Orleans Hilton and in Jackson, Lake Charles, and Bossier City are run through contract part-

In July 2007, Drago's partnered with the New Orleans Hilton Riverside to open a second Drago's restaurant.

nerships. Tommy also has his eye on further expansion opportunities.

The big question is, how does Tommy keep from over-extending himself?

"You learn from your experiences," he said. "I want to grow and get better. So, I'll ask myself, 'This is the problem I have over here; how do I get rid of the problem?' And then I get rid of the next problem. Hotel chains are always worried about percentages and margins. Casinos, on the other hand, are competing not only for the quality restaurants but also for the gaming dollar, so those people understand that when someone comes to their restaurant and they're coming from a casino next door, if they enjoy the dinner, they'll say, 'Honey, let's come here to gamble on our next trip.' If they get a bad or average food experience, they're not going to come back. The casinos understand that Drago's is 'value-added' to their casino customers, and that will allow them to increase their percentage of new customers."

Vera Buconic Occhipinti, Klara's cousin from Croatia who helped care for Tommy and Gerry as children, said Drago's burgeoning empire is a sign of Tommy's fascination with the next big thing.

"Tommy's always had a drive, and his brain is always going and his wheels are always turning in his head," Vera said.

Good friend Albert Nicaud describes Tommy's motivation as "part of the American dream" that he inherited from his immigrant parents.

"It's the American dream, the American struggle," Nicaud said. "He's a small businessman, so what is he going to have to do to reinvent himself and make things better? Let me tell you, in 1981, Fat City was dying. Disco had kind of died out in 1979 when I got out of high school, and in 1981, a lot of places were shuttered in Fat City.

"They are a nationally known restaurant today because they worked real hard and they were generous. They gave back. After a while, you can just look at people and just know their character, their goodness, and their honesty. They're not trying to sell you something. They're not trying to take advantage of you. They just want you to enjoy a good meal and have a good time in their restaurant."

A major factor in the ongoing success of Drago's is its relationship-building. Success is not a zero-sum game.

"One thing that's different about us in the restaurant business in New Orleans is that we're a lot different than Miller, Budweiser, CVS, Walgreens, and Pepsi," Tommy said. "My best friends are restaurateurs in New Orleans. Let's talk about Acme. Do they want my market share? Damn right they do. Do I want theirs? You're damn right, I do. But at the end of the day, we respect each other, and we're friends and family. We talk about what's best for our industry and work together regularly, even though I want their market share and they want mine. Acme is arguably my main competitor, but we do things together because we're different. We're New Orleans. There's no other way to explain it. We're different."

Coca-Cola executive Rocky Weigand says he almost felt "a little disloyal" when Tommy lobbied to have him appointed to the board of the Louisiana Restaurant Association because it introduced him to a new network of friends.

"I'm in an industry that's either win or lose," Rocky said. "You either serve Coke or you serve Pepsi, and if you serve Pepsi, you're not my friend. But I was immediately impressed by the generosity of the hospitality industry in New Orleans and the willingness of

Entrepreneurs in the New Orleans restaurant business compete for the same dollar, but that doesn't stop them from being great friends.

restaurateurs to work together. There's some that probably don't get along, but that's a personality trait and not an industry trait."

One day Rocky asked Tommy how he really felt that every other restaurant was trying to replicate his charbroiled oysters recipe and boasting, "We've got the best charbroiled in town!"

"Those ought to be fighting words," Rocky said. "But Tommy told me, 'As long as oysters and the seafood industry grows, I'll grow with it. I'll get my share and probably more than my share. Not everybody's going to come to Drago's every time they go out to dinner, but if others are going to do this, I'll get more than my fair share and I'm perfectly fine with that.' As much as this family gives back, it never became just about them. It was always about the industry, serving others, nurturing hospitality, being creative and creating jobs."

How rare is that collegial feeling? When Tommy's eldest daughter Maddie got married in the middle of the COVID-19 pandemic in 2020, their wedding reception was held at Drago's in Metairie. Around the room, four local restaurants had set up tables to provide a signature dish.

"It was Mr. B's, because that's where Maddie had one of her first dates with her husband Mark, and she loved the duck spring rolls," Tommy said. "It was Popeye's fried chicken, because that's one of my favorites. Al [Copeland Jr.] sent that. Kirk Talbot sent Lucky Dogs, and Mel Ziegler sent Bud's Broiler."

Maddie's wedding rehearsal was held at Acme Oyster House. At the funeral repast for Drago in 2017, at least ten restaurants sent food to honor the Croatian patriarch of the New Orleans dining industry.

"There's no other way to explain it," Rocky said. "In New Orleans, we're different."

21

Paying It Forward

One day in late April 2020, Dr. Ronnie Lahasky, an internal medicine specialist, heard the doorbell ring at his home in Erath, Louisiana, just east of Abbeville. Erath is about 145 miles west of New Orleans.

On April 28, Lahasky and his wife Janet had lost their twenty-five-year-old son Joshua after a three-and-a-half-year battle with fibrolamellar hepatocellular carcinoma, a cancer that typically affects young adults but is so rare that only two hundred cases are diagnosed worldwide each year.

Lahasky had worked at Drago's as a waiter from 1984 to 1986 before going on to medical school. He and Tommy used to socialize after work, including one memorable—or, more accurately, forgettable—occasion when they and several other friends rented a driver and a mini-bus, stocked it with food and drinks, and drove to Mary Mahoney's Old French House Restaurant in Biloxi to visit Tommy's cousins.

"Tommy and I had some good times together, so it wasn't just work," Ronnie said. "There were some stories where he and I said, 'We heard we had a good time, but neither one of us actually remembers all of it.'"

Fast-forward nearly thirty-five years. Tommy had been alerted that Ronnie's son Joshua had passed away.

"Tommy called me and asked me for my address," Ronnie said. "And then, about two and a half hours later, Tommy and Miss Klara had driven to my house with food. It was heartwarming. That was true dedication and love for a person."

Ronnie had been so touched by his interactions with the Cvitanovich family that when he had the chance, he built his ultimate, outdoor man cave. In Louisiana, that's a 2,000-square-foot enclosed patio with every fire-breathing, cooking implement ever invented. He then set about decorating the space with memories.

On the wall are three huge murals. The mural on the left is a Bourbon Street scene that includes a restaurant by the name of "Pat O'Ronnie's." The mural on the right offers the viewer a balcony peek through a pair of French Quarter shutters to the exterior of Galatoire's, the restaurant where Ronnie proposed to his wife. The middle mural depicts downtown New Orleans, St. Louis Cathedral, Café du Monde, and a tiny restaurant, out of place in a cartographical sense but clearly front and center in Ronnie's heart: Drago's.

"I had the artist put Drago's in there because that's where I worked," Ronnie said. "Tommy had never been to my house, so I took a picture of us in front of the murals. It meant so much to me that they came all this way with gumbo, seafood pasta, and other foods. We don't even live in the same city. You wouldn't have that from any other employer. That was such a huge thing."

Stories are legion about the Cvitanoviches' unrequited, small kindnesses along the way. Kitchen manager Maria Abadie was in a pharmacy with Klara one day when the woman in front of them at the cash register—a waitress wearing the uniform of another restaurant—was crying because she couldn't afford to pay for her prescription medicine.

"Miss Klara paid for it," Maria said.

The First Commandment in the kitchen at Drago's is this: "Feed the hungry." Drago and Klara always insisted that anyone coming to their restaurant looking for something to eat would not be turned away.

"Miss Klara says if someone comes to the back door, no one goes away hungry," Maria constantly reminds her kitchen staff. "If someone asks you for something to eat, you give it to them. Nobody goes hungry because she remembers when her family didn't have food in Yugoslavia and people would give them stuff. If you're up against it, they're the first people to step in and help you. There was this one kid who couldn't afford food, and Miss Klara told his father,

The center mural in Dr. Ronnie Lahasky's enclosed patio depicts Drago's Restaurant in a location that is just a bit out of place—one block from St. Louis Cathedral. But that pride of place was what Drago's meant to Lahasky, dating back to the time he was a waiter there.

'Tell your son to come here every day, I don't care, and we'll give him something to eat.'"

Klara paid for a man's hotel room so that he would not have to sleep on the streets. She has been known to drop a big check at a church fair for a small basket of tomatoes.

"Working for them makes you even more generous," Maria

In 2020, just after their twenty-five-year-old son Joshua died of cancer, Dr. Ronnie Lahasky and his wife Janet were surprised by a condolence visit from Klara and Tommy, who drove 150 miles from Metairie to Erath, Louisiana. They posed in front of the Drago's mural.

said. "When you get a call, you become like them because they're teaching you to do that."

If truth be told, some of the stories are twenty-first-century parables.

José Rodriguez is an "expediter"—the person responsible for making sure that in the midst of the controlled chaos of the kitchen, every plate gets out to customers on time and meets their expectations.

"I'm the quarterback in the kitchen—like the bridge from the waiters and the customers to the kitchen," José said. "I once asked Maria what some of my strengths and weaknesses were, and she told me, 'You stay calm no matter what's going on.' Internally, I'm praying, and externally, I'm yelling: 'I need that catfish platter and that lobster!'"

In 2013—about ten years after he started working at Drago's—José was confronted by an unspeakable tragedy. His second daughter, five-month-old Gabriella, died of accidental asphyxia as she fell asleep in his arms.

"There was a church service that Wednesday night, and as we say in our language, 'I surrender. God, I'm learning about you. Whatever it is, I want it all,'" José said. "Pain leads to purpose. I didn't have compassion for others before that. When I came back, I told Mr. Tommy I wanted to be a pastor."

At the time, José was working at Drago's at the Hilton, so he had been away from the Metairie restaurant for several years.

"Mr. Tommy paid for my daughter's funeral, and I didn't ask him to do that," José said. "I was broken and had been on this journey. That's an example of Mr. Tommy and Miss Klara giving and being there for others in a time of suffering to comfort people. They never turn away anyone who needs a meal. It's an honor to work for someone like that."

The good works extend beyond the Drago's family. The family ethos of giving back to the community was never more evident than after Katrina, when the restaurant's staff served 77,000 free, hot meals in Metairie and New Orleans in the two months after the storm.

"It's always better to serve than to be served," Klara said. "It makes me feel terrific. I go to sleep every night with my head on the pillow, and I have no regrets. I would do it all over again."

Ron St. Pierre, the former chief sales and marketing officer at

In 2013 at St. Louis Cathedral, Klara and Drago received the Order of St. Louis Medallion for their many years of help in their home parish of St. Clement of Rome in Metairie.

Drago's, got a call one evening in April 2011 from his good friend and Marine Corps buddy, Ryan Leach, about an EF4 tornado that had just destroyed the Hillcrest subdivision in Tuscaloosa, Alabama, about a mile from Bryant-Denny Stadium. Ryan, a master gunnery sergeant, is the godfather to Ron's youngest child.

"We got hit," Ryan told him.

"So, what is it that you need?"

"Everything."

The phone went dead. Ron immediately called Tommy and said he had a friend who needed some help.

"That's all I had to say," Ron recalled. "Tommy told me to come by the restaurant."

By the time Ron got to Drago's, Tommy had loaded up several ice chests.

"They were filled with enough food to feed the entire neighborhood for an entire week," Ron said. "He got some other people together and we had $1,400 in gift cards. We showed up in Tuscaloosa twenty-seven hours later and fed the entire neighborhood for a week, and we had enough food at the end to donate to a local church."

The story comes full circle. When Ryan Leach heard about Hurricane Ida in 2021, he and ten other Marines drove to Louisiana to help Marine Corps families in Chauvin and Cut Off. They brought with them seventy-eight gallons of gas, fifty gallons of diesel, roof supplies, meal kits, and $10,000 in gift cards.

"The funny thing is, ten years later, Ryan brought me back some of my gas cans that had my name on them," Ron laughed.

At the end of their mercy mission, the ten Marines came to Drago's for a lunch before heading back.

"Ryan brought them here so they could meet Tommy," Ron said. "He told the guys, 'I want you all to meet the guy who helped me out when I needed it.' Tommy went out and shook hands with everybody."

That sense of graciousness and appreciation also applies to building a bond with Drago's staff members, whose longevity in a transitory industry speaks volumes about the respect with which they are treated.

After Hurricane Ida in 2021, when the restaurant was closed for a month to repair damages, every employee was paid full salary, including tips for the waiters.

"We decided we were going to invest in our employees," Klara said. "Good employees are very hard to come by. Some of them got as much as thirty-five dollars an hour because that was the normal amount of money they would make working in the restaurant. It took us a week to do the payroll and figure out how much each person got."

Tommy and Klara provided a similar benefit for employees during the COVID-19 pandemic in 2020, when social-distancing requirements severely impacted their business. Drago's applied for and received funding through the federal Payroll Protection Program (PPP).

"Tommy got his PPP money and went to each restaurant and said, 'Look, you all stuck with me and came back to work,' and he wrote them nice checks," said attorney Albert Nicaud. "It was not, 'Here's an opportunity for my restaurant to maybe get a little cushion.' A lot of other restaurants put that PPP money in their pockets."

"Tommy has always said that everything he gives, he gets back tenfold," said Tommy's first cousin A. J. Lulich. "He says he gets it back with interest. He's got a heart as big as all get out."

In the first weeks of the pandemic shutdown in 2020, grocery store shelves were thin because of panic buying, and Tommy could see his employees struggling just to find food and other essential supplies for their families.

"We were in the Drago's dining room, and he told me he wanted to set up a commissary where his employees could get cold cuts, ketchup, mayonnaise, bread, water—all the basic needs," Coca-Cola executive Rocky Weigand said. "He was going to buy the stuff and then sell it to his employees at his cost. He was literally saying he wanted to turn his dining room into somewhat of a grocery store. Tommy told me, 'I just can't lock my doors and act like this isn't affecting people. These people are hurting.' That's the kind of creative mind and determination of never settling that have been his driving force."

In the aftermath of Hurricane Laura in August 2020, Tommy led a caravan of Drago's staffers to Lake Charles to serve food to the residents of battered southwest Louisiana.

"Then he gets a phone call," Rocky said. "It was from the casino: 'Hey, would you like to open a restaurant here?' They went there out of their own good will because they wanted to feed people."

When Hurricane Ida slammed into South Louisiana in 2021, particularly affecting Terrebonne and Lafourche parishes west of New Orleans, Tommy organized fellow restaurateurs, his own Drago's Foundation, Coca-Cola, Rouse's, and Winn Dixie to raise more than $100,000 and distribute $100 grocery gift cards for hospitality workers in the area before Christmas.

One of the beneficiaries from Chef Ron's Gumbo Shop in Metairie sent Rocky a text: "Thanks for making the holidays a little better."

After Katrina, Drago and Klara assessed the flood damage to their parish church, St. Clement of Rome in Metairie, and came up with an innovative plan to help. Drago's traditionally was closed on Sundays, but Klara offered to open the restaurant on Palm Sunday and donate every dollar of sales—not just a percentage of sales—to the church.

"It was our parish, and they had gotten water in the church and there were no carpets, and the pews were messed up," Klara recalled. "That was our very first fundraiser. We opened the restaurant on Palm Sunday from 10:30 a.m. to 2:00 p.m., and everything that came in went to St. Clement. We do this every year now, and I think by now it's probably amounted to $400,000 or so. I remember the first year we raised $29,000."

From there, Drago's expanded its organized philanthropy to include, on an annual basis, fundraisers for St. Augustine High School and Christian Brothers School in New Orleans. Drago's regularly holds fund-raisers for the families of fallen police officers.

Beyond generating goodwill among the wider community, the generosity produced tangible results for the schools and for the restaurant.

"It gave us a big lift up because our business got better," Klara said. "You've never seen an advertisement for Drago's Restaurant in the paper. We advertise by giving away."

The list of charitable causes grows every year. After Katrina, the restaurant celebrated its patriarch Drago's birthday by raising thousands of dollars for an affordable housing effort called the St. Bernard Project, which coordinated the construction of three homes for hospitality workers after the BP oil spill in 2010, and for Second Harvest Food Bank of Greater New Orleans and Acadiana, which serves those who need food in twenty-three civil parishes of South Louisiana.

For several years, Drago's delivered forty meals every Wednesday to a New Orleans nursing home. Drago's has been a staple at parish fairs at St. Clement of Rome, St. Catherine of Siena, and St. Philip Neri Catholic churches and offered thousands of dollars in gift certificates to help nonprofit fund-raisers.

Johnny Matesich, Tommy's cousin whose uncle, Johnny Gentilich, ran the Marble Hall Saloon at 720 Lafayette Street across from Gallier Hall in the 1950s, said the desire to offer help comes from a fundamental place in the heart. Drago and Klara were immigrants with meager financial means, he said, and they always remembered how fortunate they were, especially after Katrina.

"The first thing that comes to your mind is, 'Oh, they did it so people would become their friends and come to their restaurant,'" Johnny said. "No! They didn't do it for that. They did it because they wanted to help. They were there to help the people. They didn't expect anything in return. They did it from the bottom of their hearts, because that's in their DNA. And Drago and Klara ingrained that in Tommy and Gerry, and they're the same way. They're giving people. They're first in line and they say, 'We're all in!'"

The family estimates that its total giving to schools, churches, and other charitable causes has amounted to $5 million over the last twenty years. That doesn't even count the times Drago's has stepped in when a fellow restaurateur has suffered a disaster. When fire destroyed Gendusa's Restaurant in Kenner in 2020, Drago's delivered tables and chairs to help it get back on its feet.

In 2011, Tommy was awarded the prestigious Loving Cup, presented by the *Times-Picayune* since 1901 to a person who has performed heroic community service without any expectation of

At Christmastime in 2009, Tommy and his crew of Santa's helpers drove the Drago's firetruck to Padua House in Belle Chasse, a Catholic Charities program that cares for the intellectually and developmentally disabled. (Photo by Frank J. Methe, Clarion Herald)

Santa Cvitanovich dropped off some early Christmas presents to the residents of Padua House. (Photo by Frank J. Methe, Clarion Herald*)*

recognition. The award was given to him at St. Clement of Rome, the church his restaurant helped restore after Katrina.

"This is actually the honor of a lifetime," Tommy told a church packed with family, friends, and restaurant colleagues. "It still hasn't sunk in completely. This is not about me. It's about everyone around me. We do this together."

At the awards celebration, Leah Chase, the grand dame of New

Orleans Creole cooking who previously had received the Loving Cup, reflected on how the Cvitanovich family rallied to her aid after Katrina to assist in rebuilding her Dooky Chase Restaurant in Treme, which had been looted and swallowed up by five feet of water. Tommy was floored by Chase's gratitude.

"To see an icon of our industry—and to help her out—was one of the proudest moments of my life," Tommy said.

And then he turned to his parents, sitting in the front pew.

"My parents have had such a positive impact on so many lives," Tommy said. "I don't think my dad realizes how important his name is in this community. Hearing the name 'Drago' is synonymous with service—service to customers and service to fellow man."

22
"Hey, Mr. Tommy"

If there has been a "sea change" in the operational structure of Drago's—transforming itself from the mom-and-pop seafood eatery of a half-century ago into the seven-and-counting, modern restaurants that comprise Drago's charbroiled oyster empire today—technology has been at the helm.

Only half-jokingly, Tommy says his mother controls the checkbook: "She still signs my checks."

That is true. Klara, in fact, does sign paper checks at her desk every day. Tommy nurtures his parents' core values of treating employees with honor and respect and creates a menu that delivers great food, at great prices, that people want to eat.

But just about everything else regarding Drago's operational structure has changed from its mom-and-pop beginnings.

In place today are sophisticated software systems unheard of in the 1970s, when waiters scribbled orders in small notebooks with pencils (if they even bothered to write the orders down) and carried them from the table to the back of the house.

For years, in her role as the perpetually vigilant hostess at the front door, Klara used paper and pencil to scribble down table assignments for waiters. That arrangement would work perfectly fine today, Klara says, but Tommy convinced her to look to the horizon and accept the introduction of Open Table software, which essentially does the same thing she did with her number two lead pencil.

"Let's face it, I'm not going to be here forever, and I want the restaurant to succeed," Klara said.

The business software now in place gives Klara a 360-degree, real-time view of how each of her restaurants is performing. It's light-years removed from the times in the 1960s when Drago Batinich, who ran the original Drago's restaurant in Lakeview, kept "all of his bookkeeping in his pocket."

"I get a report every day from all of our restaurants that breaks down our sales in categories like liquor, beer, wine, food," Klara said. "Alcohol is always the thing that makes you money."

In the "good old days," Klara would complete all of the weekly accounting herself on Sundays—one reason Drago's in Metairie carried on its menus the therapeutic advisory, "Never on Sunday."

"Sunday was for us," Klara said. "We went to church on Sunday, and then on Sunday afternoon, we went out with the kids for a little while, and then on Sunday night, I did the books. I used to do it every night, and then on Sunday night, I finished the week. As long as I had money to pay my bills, I was happy. The way I used to work it was that if I was out of money, I would stop buying whatever. But I always made sure that my main bills—electricity, rent and the note on the restaurant—were paid before anything else. It was not an easy go."

Today, Klara scans her emails and social media posts from customers every morning, a practice that helps her measure her patrons' enjoyment level. Klara's granddaughter Maddie Cvitanovich Tinney showed her one comment recently that tickled her: "This elderly, sweet lady treated us so nicely."

"She said 'elderly'—she didn't say 'old,'" Klara said, laughing. "I check all of the emails in the morning. You have to investigate if there is a problem and, if you can, call and apologize. I'm happy when I see 'five stars' in the morning when I get up. If it's a bad one, I get upset.

"The secret calculus of a restaurant's success continues to be eternal vigilance," Klara says. "Nothing can tell a restaurant owner more than visiting with customers and gently probing with them whether or not everything was to their satisfaction.

"It's important to walk around because if something is wrong, you can right on the spot correct it," Klara said. "If someone says, 'Oh, two of my oysters were dry and I couldn't eat them,' I get them two oysters. Whatever might be the case. If they don't tell me, I can't correct it. I always tell everyone, from our managers down to the bussers and the food runners, 'If we don't have teamwork, we're going to fail.'"

Tommy says it is vital for a restaurant to learn from its shortcomings.

"You learn from your mistakes," he said. "When people send emails that say, 'Oh, it was wonderful, it was great,' I don't read those too much. When I get a negative one, I read it because that's what makes us better. When people tell me, 'Everything was perfect,' I don't really want to hear that. I'll ask them, 'Well, what was the *least* perfect?' What my dad taught me—and this is something I should do more of—was to watch the plates when they come back into the kitchen. What are our customers not eating? They just paid for it, and they're not eating it. There might be a few reasons: Maybe it didn't taste good, or maybe it's not appealing, or maybe it doesn't look good. Or maybe they're too full and there's too much food on the plate."

Klara admits she has mellowed from the early days of restaurant ownership when her exactitude and her expectations for perfection may have triggered her to lose her temper. Drago could get testy, as well, when something wasn't right.

"I believe anybody who wants their job to last appreciates being corrected," Klara said. "Every now and then, I will pull someone to the side and say, 'That was not right,' or I'll see water on the floor, which creates a danger for someone to slip. The rule is whoever passes by the water first has to pick up the water right away.

"Everybody respects me. They know I'm looking. Everybody who works here gets a check, and my signature is on that check. The majority of them think I'm nice. Some people in the kitchen might be a little more scared of me, but I have mellowed. You really have to be 'silk gloves' now."

The secret to creating a good working environment, Tommy says, is to be clear on the expectations for every employee.

"We all have issues," Tommy said. "But I tell them: 'When you walk into the restaurant, you leave your issues and your problems outside. Come inside and enjoy yourself at work, because I promise you one more thing, when you step out the door and that doorknob hits you in the tail, that problem is going to be waiting for you. You're going to be here forty-fifty hours a week. So while you're here, have fun and enjoy yourself. If you're not happy, that stuff spreads. It's contagious. Plus, I don't want to hear your problems. I like you, but I've got my own problems.' Customers can sense if a server or a bartender shows their personal life via their attitude."

Kitchen manager Freddie McKnight said he has learned in more than three decades of working elbow-to-elbow with Tommy how important it is not to pontificate but to lead by example.

"Tommy told me something a long time ago—that you can't walk around swinging a big stick and demanding stuff," Freddie said. "You treat people how you want to be treated. If you treat people with respect, then you will get respect. I'm not going to ask you to do nothing that I wouldn't do myself or haven't done myself. The key is respect."

There are days when Freddie comes to work and the kitchen is close to being overwhelmed.

"I'm not a manager who's going to stand by the wall and say, 'Do this, do that,'" Freddie said. "I'll throw an apron on. I had a guy who started in the kitchen, and it took him about a month to realize I was a manager. He thought I was a line cook. When I walk in and they're busy, it's like, 'Good morning, everybody! Where do you need me at?' Tommy could get back on the line today. If he sees the kitchen struggling, he can get back there and help."

The revolutionary technology of point-of-sale (POS) restaurant software—Drago's uses systems called "POSitouch" and "Toast"—has created a seamless table-to-kitchen-to-table process. The system prints out full tickets—sometimes even printing separate tickets for individual cooking stations—as well as displays an electronic version for real-time viewing in the kitchen.

"It's amazing when you think back to even thirty years ago when we didn't have a POS system and we were hand-writing tickets and adding up the checks on an adding machine, and then you think about the system we have now and how it's progressed," Tommy says. "Toast takes the same POS technology and integrates it with your credit card information. We capture your credit card information when you're paying a bill, and the payment gets deposited. Your credit card doesn't leave the table. The POS system is now your credit card processor.

"Probably the most confusing item for a restaurateur to shop, period, is credit card processing fees, because one person might come in with a debit card, another person with a regular credit card, another with a rewards card, another with a super rewards card, another with American Express—and each card has a different rate and sometimes a transaction fee. That tells me the banks are 'making bank' on credit card processing, because the more confused they make it, the better it is for them. I don't *struggle* to figure it out—I *can't* figure it out."

One thing Tommy absolutely has figured out is the way a plate moves through the byzantine laboratory of the kitchen.

"Flow is everything," he said. "Everything needs to work toward the door to go out to the dining room. I go crazy in the kitchen—whether we're doing a banquet or whether we're just pushing orders out—when a plate goes backwards. Everything needs to work its way out."

Kitchen equipment has become so high-tech that certain pots used to create soups and gumbo have a built-in scale that can measure the weight of the liquid gold, guaranteeing a specific and consistent flavor profile from day to day.

"I never thought about putting a scale on the bottom of a pot," Tommy said.

Tommy would not be surprised one day to see more restaurants transitioning to an electronic menu—such as is currently in use at airport cafes—so that customers can look at pictures of a prospective dish before they order.

"Now, when you go to places like Emeril's, Galatoire's, Commander's—take your pick—you're not expecting someone to be there with an iPad," Tommy said. "You're expecting, in some cases, for the waiter to remember everything. Let's face it. At Galatoire's, the customers go crazy if they change the ice they use in the glasses. That's the importance of sticking to tradition for an iconic New Orleans restaurant.

"But it's a big topic right now—do restaurants put pictures on their menus? When people see pictures on a menu, they automatically think of Denny's or Waffle House or Asian restaurants. You would never see it at Commander's, Galatoire's or Emeril's, but it's a big conversation because people are saying pictures would help sell. Before long, you're going to see this because customers are pretty much going to demand it. But then you've got people like myself—we're going to fight it as long as we can."

No matter how electronically advanced a restaurant is, Tommy says success comes down to nurturing and maintaining quality employees and using common sense. Many years ago, the restaurant installed TVs to allow customers to follow the latest news and sports, but Tommy realizes that, especially in today's polarized political climate, he has to maintain a level playing field.

"Roughly half of my customers are Democrats and half are Republicans," he says. "Democrats and Republicans both eat oysters. We've got customers who are conservative and liberal. We've got customers of all races. You have stay so Switzerland that it's not even funny. You got to be even fairer than Switzerland, and we are."

That extends to the TV channels that are displayed in every Drago's restaurant.

"We have a policy: If you have FOX on one TV, you'd better have CNN on the other," Tommy said. "We have two TVs in our Baton Rouge restaurant—the 'CNN' TV and the 'FOX' TV. And every week or two, we rotate them. People notice that."

People also notice that the Cvitanovich family is always present, minding the store. That means something.

"People who are successful in any business they pursue are 100 percent dedicated and in love with their business," said Dr. Ronnie Lahasky, a former Drago's waiter. "When you see the owners of the restaurant at the restaurant, it's going to do very well. Miss Klara and Mr. Drago were always there, and Tommy is always there."

Success has bred success.

"We've won a lot of championships together, and we've worked years together," said long-time expediter José Rodriguez. "New people come and go, but there's a core of us who have worked together for two decades. We trust each other in those high-pressure situations."

Maybe it goes back to the desire Drago and Klara held deeply in their hearts when they arrived in the U.S.

Failure was not an option.

"It was just a mentality," Tommy's cousin A. J. Lulich said. "If you have no safety net, you have to be successful. I mean, you've got no choice. You're walking a tightrope without a net."

Tommy has never been a celebrity chef. He prefers to celebrate his family's improbable journey.

"We are who we are," Tommy says. "Yeah, we work hard. Yeah, we got some recipes. Yeah, we had some friends and got some breaks. But at the end of the day, we are who we are because of our employees. At the end of the day, I demand respect, a safe working environment, and being polite. I learned quite some time ago that everybody puts their pants on the same way. Everybody's got the same kind of blood that runs through their veins."

One of Tommy's favorite long-time employees is Mark Eiserloh, who has special needs. Mark's mother often ate at the restaurant and asked Tommy one day if there might be a job that her son could do. Mark has worked part-time for thirty years. There are several other employees with special needs.

"I tell people all the time, 'You realize your day's not that bad when Mark walks up to you and says, 'Hey, Mr. Tommy, how are you doing?'" Tommy said.

For her birthday one year, Mark gave kitchen manager Maria Abadie a colorful card with a handwritten note.

"I told Tommy, 'See, this is why I work here,'" Maria said. "It touches your heart."

23
"Make My Day"

The "NOLA No-Call" changed everything.

When the New Orleans Saints were assigned the role of sacrificial lamb in what may have been the worst "no-call" in NFL history—a blatant pass interference committed by Los Angeles Rams cornerback Nickell Robey-Coleman that was not flagged in the final minute of the NFC Championship Game on January 20, 2019, costing the Saints a certain berth in their second Super Bowl—black-and-gold fans became apoplectic with rage.

That the NFL ultimately admitted—eight days later—that the referee crew had made an egregious oversight did nothing to salve the righteous anger of the Who Dat Nation.

At noon on February 3, 2019, with most of America settling down to their nachos and watch parties for Super Bowl LIII between the Rams and the New England Patriots, the entire population of Greater New Orleans, it seemed, descended on Decatur Street in front of Jackson Square.

Tens of thousands of Saints fans with every justifiable reason to be paranoid (see: "Bountygate" and the one-year suspension of coach Sean Payton in 2012) had a singular mission. They were there to launch a "NOLA No-Call Day of Mourning" second line because in their measured opinion, Super Bowl "LIII"—literally and figuratively—was Super Bowl "LIE."

In the New Orleans jazz funeral tradition, the second line began with slow-cadenced dirges. Fans dressed as refs wore Coke-bottle glasses and probed for potholes in the asphalt with white canes. Revelers showcased a "toe-heel" dance step as they rhythmically moved down Decatur. As the teeming procession hit Canal Street and turned right, New Orleans showed why it is New Orleans and not Detroit, where people have been known to burn cars and sofas after *winning* a title.

At the intersection of Canal and Bourbon streets, a man dressed in an Alvin Kamara number forty-one jersey led the crowd in a Gospel-like, call-and-response that showed why New Orleans is different than any other place on earth:

"Who got *rah-ahb'd?*"
"We got robbed!"
"Who got *rah-ahb'd?*"
"We got robbed!"

The sheer joy of the Saints' crowd was exceeded only by what happened eight hours later: Patriots 13, Rams 3.

The tentacles of the NOLA No-Call extended to Drago's. When NFL executives considered the health and safety of their officiating crews going forward for the 2019 regular season and beyond, they decided that when the Saints played a home game, it would be better for the officiating crew to stay at a Metairie hotel rather than in downtown New Orleans, where the night before the game they might run into lots of Saints' fans with amazingly short-term memories.

New Orleanian Tony Meyer, a college football referee, helped the NFL work its way out of a potentially sticky situation.

"The refs were in a Metairie hotel, and they were looking for somewhere to eat," Tony said. "I told them, 'I've got a great place for you.' So I called Tommy. He doesn't take reservations, but he said, 'I'm going to do you one better.' He's got a man cave in his restaurant, like a conference room. Normally, when those guys go out to eat at a restaurant, they stick out like a sore thumb because you see ten guys at dinner, and nobody's drinking. Tommy was kind enough to put them in the conference room, and, man, they loved it."

From that initial experience in 2019, NFL crews coming to New Orleans to work Saints' home games were hypnotically drawn to the smoke signals from the charbroiled oyster grill: Drago's was the place to eat.

"Out of the ten home games every season, we probably have the refs here eight times," Tommy said.

There are two postscripts that apply to the feeding of the NFL refs the night before the game:

First, Bill Vinovich, the crew chief for the NOLA No-Call, actually is Croatian, a revelation that has caused some genetic consternation among the Cvitanovich clan.

"You sure he's not Serbian?" Tommy's cousin A. J. Lulich laughed.

"I don't get into all of that," Tommy said. "Was I teed off? Yeah. Did we get screwed? Yeah. But when the refs come in, they talk like regular customers. They talk sports. They talk family. They're not having a meeting. The crews are very thankful. I often get thank-you notes from them."

Second, in a nod to common sense—and that decision may change with the passage of time—the NFL has not assigned Vinovich to referee a Saints' home game since the infamous no-call in 2019.

"He won't be back here again," Tony Meyer said flatly. "They're not going to send him back here because he was the face of the crew, and everybody thinks he was responsible for not making the call."

When Klara was in the travel agency business, she had the Saints as one of her marquee clients.

"We would know about the Saints' roster transactions before anyone in the media knew," Tommy said.

The elder Drago, who played semi-professional soccer in Yugoslavia, also was an enormous sports fan, traveling twice with his son Gerry to the World Cup—to Los Angeles in 1994 and to France in 1998. As a newly minted physician, Gerry was finally in a financial position in 1994 to fulfill one of his dad's dreams—seeing a World Cup final in person, when Brazil faced Italy in the championship match in California.

"He just loved it," Gerry recalled. "I remember walking up to the Rose Bowl in Pasadena, and he's got a Croatian flag draped over his shoulders, and I remember thinking, 'This is so silly.' But I'll be damned, you get to the stadium and there's people from all over the world with their country's flags draped over them. Tickets for the World Cup Championship were ridiculously expensive, but I was going to make sure that he had great seats. I paid $1,100 per ticket, but it was worth it. I was just starting to make money, and I had to swallow hard to pay that much, but I'm glad I paid it. We were

Gerry bought prime tickets to take his dad to the 1994 World Cup at the Rose Bowl in Pasadena, California.

Drago touted Croatian wine as a true gift of the gods, although former LSU basketball coach Press Maravich, a Serbian, used to provoke Klara's mother when she was tending bar.

thirty rows up. It was incredible. The game finished in a tie, and the penalty kicks to determine the winner were right in front of us."

Let the record show that Brazil beat Italy with a 3-2 edge in the penalty shootout.

Drago's favorite "American" sport, Klara said, was basketball, and that love of roundball brought him into frequent contact with LSU coach Press Maravich and his All-America and future NBA All-Star son, "Pistol Pete" Maravich. Press was a Serb, but the centuries of enmity between the Croats and Serbs simply melted away at the oyster bar at Drago's, where Klara's mother Marija helped out when she was visiting New Orleans.

"He used to come in at a time when we had Yugoslavian food on the menu," Klara recalled. "Press used to come to the restaurant all the time because he had some Croatian players from Chicago. He would come up to the bar and tease my mom, 'Give me a glass of that wonderful, sweet Serbian wine!' And my mom felt like throwing something at him. He always wanted my mom to respond. She just covered it up. She was a good actor."

Later, Drago and Klara became close friends with Press Maravich's successor—Dale Brown, who always had his eye on young basketball talent in Yugoslavia. Brown brought over six-foot-four guard Nebojsa Bukumirovich and, later, seven-foot-one center Zoran Jovanovich, both natives of Belgrade and both Serbs.

"Every weekend we would have them here," Klara said. "When Zoran had a surgery for a knee injury, he stayed in Tommy's house for a month and a half."

In the late 1980s, Dale Brown's wife Vonnie, an international dance instructor, and several dozen women of Croatian descent would come to Drago's on Sundays when the restaurant was closed to practice for a fundraiser to benefit the United Slavonian Benevolent Association (USBA). That group was formed in 1874 to help care for Croatian American orphans and widows and also defray the cost of funeral expenses for members of the community.

Drago was a major cheerleader for the ethnic association, which prided itself on self-help. Members of the USBA emphasized the importance of never having to rely on outside support in a time of need—a trait that held true after Katrina.

"We took no local, state or federal aid during the hardest times, including the Great Depression," Drago explained to a reporter in 1989. "In that respect, we have lived up to the bylaws and obligations set down by our ancestors. I liked the philosophy: 'Love one another.'"

There is little question the family's love of sports also was beneficial in expanding the restaurant's reach. After Katrina, at the behest of new Saints coach Sean Payton, Drago's began feeding the entire team and office staff at their practice facility on Airline Drive every Friday afternoon during the NFL season.

Tommy dubbed it "Football Fridays."

"We'll cook maybe 1,500 to 2,000 oysters for them on a Friday," Tommy said.

The relationship between the Saints and Drago's blossomed in the spring of 2006, just six months after Katrina. Payton selected

Drago's—not an elegantly appointed place such as Galatoire's or Commander's Palace—as the restaurant where he would make the hard sell to a free-agent quarterback coming off major rotator-cuff surgery.

That quarterback was Drew Brees.

How'd that work out exactly for New Orleans?

Brees, who is allergic to dairy, gluten, and nuts, ordered his charbroiled oysters without the cheese. Brees fell in love with Drago's to the extent that he and his wife Brittany became regular customers and were, in a sense, welcomed into the Drago's family. In 2021, Brees capped off his future Pro Football Hall of Fame career by celebrating his retirement with Brittany at Drago's.

The charbroiled oysters, with no cheese, had come full circle.

"We were honored that he did that because he didn't talk about a lot of other places," Klara said. "Whenever he came, we tried to give him a good table—some place in the corner—and sometimes we put them in Tommy's office."

The NFL, which conducts surveys on just about anything that moves, seeks feedback from every team each year about the best and the worst aspects of road travel—including hotel accommodations, bus service to and from the airport, security details, and, yes, food. After nearly every Saints' home game, Drago's serves a post-game meal to players and coaches of the visiting team. The team first goes through a pop-up, TSA luggage check in a secured area of the Superdome, and then sits down for a Drago's-supplied meal. After they eat, the players board buses to the airport.

"That's so they can get right on their plane," Tommy said.

The ultimate affirmation of success is the number of NFL teams that specifically request Drago's to serve their post-game meal at the Superdome.

"Every year, the NFL gets all the trip planners and dieticians together for a meeting, and they compare the services they received from the hotels and what rental company they used for massage tables, what police department they used for escort, who served them their meals—and they grade them," Tommy said. "We don't get to see the reports, but I've always been told that we're probably the best in the NFL. You can't buy that. You work hard to earn that."

Charbroiled oysters are always on the post-game menu after games, Tommy says. But just as Brees has certain dietary musts, so did Tampa Bay quarterback Tom Brady.

"Brady had a set menu of nuts and grains," Tommy said. "We always work with the team dietician. They'll pick what they want for most of the players, and then there are certain players that have certain diets, so we'll have to follow that, whether it's vegan or whatever. It's usually pre-boxed."

There is only one regular Saints' opponent that Drago's does not serve—the Atlanta Falcons. That's not exactly an indication of animus toward the Falcons; it's that Messina's has had that business and always does a great job.

"Actually, it makes me happy, because I don't like the Falcons!" Tommy said, laughing.

In 2003, Tommy's friend Bob DeViney came to him and David Blitch, an executive with the Hilton New Orleans Riverside, and pitched an idea that would give New Orleans' annual PGA golf tournament a distinctive flavor: Put ten of the city's best restaurants under a "Champions Club" tent to the left of the eighteenth hole and let them offer a special dish to patrons eager to experience great golf and great food. The money raised would go to the tournament's non-profit charities as well as to culinary educational programs sponsored by the Louisiana Restaurant Association.

"When Bob came to me with the idea, I said, 'Dude, there's no way that's going to work,'" Tommy recalled.

Tommy's not wrong often, but in this case, he was. The Champions Club became one of the premier amenities on the PGA Tour, subsequently copied by many others.

"It became the talking point of just about every golf tournament," Tommy said. "Here we are on the fairway of the eighteenth hole and everybody's going, 'Quiet, please! Quiet, please!' and yet we're partying and drinking and cutting up. The PGA wasn't used to it. Other cities have had a hard time duplicating the Champions Club for one reason: they don't have the restaurants we have."

Less than a month after Phil Mickelson won his first major championship—the Masters in 2004—Mickelson came to English Turn and finished second by one shot to Vijay Singh in the Zurich

Classic. Carrying a platter of charbroiled oysters, Tommy kept trying to get into the players-only clubhouse to give Mickelson a taste test.

His wheels were always turning.

"Tommy was on a mission to get those dozen charbroiled in front of Phil because he wanted Phil to taste it and make that a dish for the Masters Champions Dinner the next year," said Acme Oyster House owner Mike Rodrigue.

Even though Tommy didn't succeed in getting the charbroiled oysters on the Masters Champions Dinner menu, word of Drago's spread so fast among the Zurich field that dozens come to the restaurant during tournament week. Tommy usually gets his five-plus minutes of fame describing his oysters on the Golf Channel to a worldwide audience.

"I think it's honestly the single best bite of seafood there is," Mike Rodrigue said, "and I think if you served it without the oyster but just the butter and seasonings, it would be pretty damn good, too."

Looking back at all the celebrities who have walked through the doors of Drago's in Metairie—Shaquille O'Neal, Brad Pitt, Angelina Jolie, the late Supreme Court Chief Justice Antonin Scalia, Sean Payton, Drew Brees, Britney Spears—the Drago's staff will always remember the sparkling elegance of the distinguished former mayor of Carmel, California.

Try having Clint Eastwood walk into your restaurant and order tomato juice—and the only thing you have on hand is Zing Zang Bloody Mary Mix.

"We had to go out and get tomato juice for him," said Ivana Popich, front of the house manager.

Make my day.

Drago's did.

24
"Living the American Dream"

Even as his physical and mental health waned in the months before his death, Drago Cvitanovich remained present to his family through the many gifts that had punctuated a remarkable life—his ready smile and his resonant baritone voice. Despite the progression of Drago's dementia, Gerry said one of the miracles of his final days was that he never forgot his immediate family.

When he was riding herd at the restaurant in his earlier years, Drago loved to sing, so much so that he would race to a table whenever he discovered a patron was celebrating a birthday to orchestrate the staff's singing of "Happy Birzzday." Every year on Christmas Eve, the extended Cvitanovich family would gather at Klara and Drago's house not far from the restaurant, and Drago would proudly conduct his clan in the singing of Christmas carols and Croatian folk songs.

"He loved singing happy birthday so much that he even sang it to Jesus on Christmas Eve!" Gerry said.

"Drago had a beautiful voice," said restaurant manager Ivana Popich, who, while not being a blood relative, said Drago always teased her at the end of his life that "I was the daughter he never had."

One Croatian tradition at Christmas, especially in Drago's fishing village of Igrane, is the *"badnjak"*: the family gathers at the hearth, and a male member of the family throws a Yule log on the fire while Christmas carols are intoned.

In 2016, Drago's grandniece Deša—the little girl from Dubrovnik who took her first steps on the bar at Drago's during the Croatian war—visited New Orleans again and knew that the family patriarch was nearing the end of his life.

"When I was saying goodbye to him, he was quiet because he

A Croatian tradition at Christmas is called the "badnjak," where the family gathers at the hearth, and a male member of the family throws a Yule log on the fire while everyone sings Christmas carols.

Drago led the singing at the traditional Croatian Yule log ceremony.

was dealing with dementia," Deša recalled. "When I said goodbye to him, I was crying because I didn't know if I was going to see him again. He said, 'Baby, if you need anything, just let us know.' He was always like that—'If you ever need anything, just let me know. We are here for you.'"

Father Joseph Krafft, a Catholic priest and a close family friend during his time serving as a parochial vicar at St. Clement of Rome Church in Metairie, says what struck him about the Cvitanovich family during Drago's final months was how they joined hands and grew even closer.

"Klara and the family never considered a nursing home," Father Krafft said. "They opted instead to have friends and family sit with Drago throughout the day, and Klara cared for him at night after working twelve hours-plus at the restaurant. If someone had walked into their house then, they likely would not have realized the proximity of Drago's death. That's because Klara joyfully attended to the needs of her ailing husband."

Even from his bed at home, Father Krafft said Drago would "pass many hours of the day singing to Klara." The priest felt privileged to be a part of the family's bedside vigil near the end.

"Their gathering was not so much in quiet sadness but more like a celebration of a life well-lived," he said. "There were a lot of touching stories that were filled with love, joy, and hope for Drago's eternal reward. I've attended many of these bedside vigils, but it's very rare to see an entire family of kids and grandkids gathered on the bed and all around the room, sharing in such a melancholic moment."

Klara and her children made sure to play Drago's two favorite songs over and over at his bedside—"Marijana" and "Adio Mare." He would sing along happily until the day before he died.

Klara and Drago's immigration journey—arriving in New Orleans with three suitcases, two boys, and a pocketful of dreams—is memorialized in Franco Alessandrini's white Carrara marble *Monument to the Immigrant,* erected in 1995 at Woldenberg Park on the Mississippi River.

The marble figures of a husband, wife, and their two children are not Klara, Drago, Tommy, and Gerry—those sculpted figures represent all immigrants as an archetype—but the inscription at the base of the monument plaque sums up the Cvitanoviches' immigration

Drago and his beloved Croatian flag were never far apart. He loved returning with his family to the waters of Croatia every summer.

story in thirty-seven words: "Drago and Klara Cvitanovich immigrated from Croatia in June (1961), with a vision that only hard work and perseverance could make happen. What they gave to their sons and others is an example for generations to follow."

Brittney Montes de Oca, who was Drago's nurse in the ICU stepdown unit at East Jefferson General Hospital in his final days, said she used the quiet time to reflect on her years of interacting with Drago when she was a waitress at the restaurant.

She recalled as Drago was getting frailer but still coming to the restaurant, Klara would drive close to the front entrance. Brittney would meet Drago at the door, escort him slowly to his favorite chair at the bar and get him a cup of coffee with cream and sugar.

"He didn't know it was decaf," Brittney said.

When Drago died at home on February 4, 2017, Brittney went to Facebook to share her love for someone who had become like a grandfather to her: "The world lost the most gentle soul today, but heaven gained the most beautiful angel. Rest in peace, sweet Drago. You will be dearly missed more than you could have ever known."

Tommy knew his father's funeral would be a hero's sendoff. After all, in Drago and Klara's more than half-century in New Orleans, their story had become an inspirational touchstone validating the value of hard work and generosity.

In 2014, Drago and Klara had been inducted into the Louisiana Restaurant Association's Hall of Fame and also received the Ella Brennan Lifetime Achievement Award from the New Orleans Wine and Food Experience. A year earlier, the Louisiana Hospitality Foundation honored Drago's charitable passion by creating the Drago Cvitanovich Award for outstanding philanthropy by an entrepreneur.

But not even Tommy was prepared for the outpouring of love from friends—and strangers—who had benefited from an American dream realized. The night before the funeral, the line of cars trying to reach the Lake Lawn Metairie Funeral Home for the wake was so long it caused a traffic jam at the Metairie Road exit off I-10.

On the day of Drago's funeral, Klara, Tommy, Gerry and their entire families were at St. Clement of Rome Church at 8:00 a.m. to receive the body.

"There were literally a dozen Orleans and Jefferson parish motorcycles and two police cars that escorted my dad," Tommy said.

"The funeral was like a who's who of New Orleans," Father Krafft said.

Tommy, Gerry, and attorney Albert Nicaud eulogized Drago. Albert told the story about Drago chasing out the sour-faced customer who had complained about a baby crying at the next table. Drago had zero patience for someone who didn't like kids. He cherished the family-building that occurred around the family table.

Klara and Drago's immigration journey is reflected in Franco Alessandrini's white Carrara marble Monument to the Immigrant.

"Drago understood that having a successful restaurant was not only about good food and service but also about relationships," Albert said. "Everyone who walked through the door got greeted with, 'Hi, nice to see you! Thank you for coming to my restaurant!' He was truly appreciative of everybody who walked through the door, and you could feel it."

At the end of the Funeral Mass, instead of going directly to

Lake Lawn Metairie Cemetery, the police motorcycle escort took a specially tailored route: the officers drove east on West Esplanade Avenue toward Lakeside Shopping Center and then took a right on North Arnoult Road, which in the early 1960s was a shell road.

Drago was making his final farewell to the restaurant he had built with his wife through their Croatian willpower and their shared faith in each other.

As the black hearse pulled slowly into the parking lot, crawling to a stop, dozens of Drago's employees in their black uniforms stepped forward and placed a single red rose on top.

"It was very emotional," waitress Nancy Fish said. "It was a wonderful feeling, but a sad feeling to lose Drago. It was glorious because he paraded in front of his restaurant one last time. He came real slow so everybody could say their goodbyes."

In the summer of 2017, just a few months after Drago passed away, the Cvitanovich family and relatives—about eighty in all—made their annual pilgrimage back to Croatia. This trip, of course, was packed with raw emotions. To accommodate everyone, the family chartered two large yachts, which each had twenty cabins, to sail to several ports of special significance to Drago.

One of the ports of call, of course, was Drago's hometown of Igrane. Family and friends made their way to the top of a hill to the small church where Drago's parents were buried. The churches of Croatia are packed every Sunday—the result of an entire country having lost its ability to worship for a half-century—but this memorial was a private, Croatian American moment.

Before Drago died, Tommy and Gerry had clipped a lock of their father's hair and placed it in a plastic bag.

"The main reason I chose to do that was that at the end of his life, he regularly asked for his mom, and I knew we would be going back there soon," Tommy said.

In the cemetery of the small mountainside Church of St. Michael overlooking Igrane, Tommy eulogized his father. Tommy's son Josh brushed aside the pebbles in front of Drago's parents' grave and placed some of Drago's hair in the tiny hole he had dug.

Later, on the shore of the Adriatic Sea, Gerry told his family and friends another story. On a visit to Igrane, Drago had grown tired of

After Drago's funeral Mass in 2017, the hearse bearing his casket drove from St. Clement of Rome Church in Metairie for one last stop at the restaurant he founded in 1971.

Drago's staff members lined up to say a final prayer and place a red rose on his hearse.

seven-year-old Gerry playing in the shallow water and refusing to swim.

"So, he took me to the deep-water pier, where the water was probably thirty feet deep, tied a rope around my waist and threw me in the water," Gerry said. "I was screaming."

Gerry's cries were so panicked, Tommy said, that a lady watching the episode unfold said, "Call the police on this man!"

"It was a bad daddy moment," Tommy said, laughing, "but Gerry learned how to swim."

From that same pier about fifty years later, Gerry held up another lock of Drago's hair and tied a piece of string around it. He then threw Drago's hair into the water—and then jumped in after it, feet first.

Gerry survived—again.

On a night near the end of the pilgrimage, the Cvitanoviches disembarked from the yacht. There were three small boats moored side by side. As the family walked the dock on their way to a seaside dinner, the boat next to theirs was playing soft music.

It was the Croatian folk song that Drago had loved above all others: "Marijana." It's the same song that little Deša—the baby who took her first steps on the Drago's bar in 1991 and who was now thirty—sang for Teta Klara in 2021.

"As Drago's dementia had progressed, he would come to parties in his wheelchair, and he loved to sing 'Marijana,'" Albert Nicaud said. "'Marijana' is a love story about a sailor who had to go away to sea, and he had lost the love of his life, Marijana." It goes:

> On one wonderful, silent May night
> You told me you'd come on our first rendezvous
> Night is around me, there is darkness everywhere
> But Marijana is sleeping alone
> And she doesn't know I'm here
> Sweet little Marijana [*Slatka, mala Marijana*]
> But I'm sitting alone under the palm tree
> And a dream is closing my eyes and I'm sad
> I'm waiting for the long desired day
> Oh Marijana, sweet little Marijana
> I will wait for you till morning light
> Oh Marijana, sweet little Marijana
> I will wait for you because you will come.

On an extended family summer trip to Croatia after Drago's death in 2017, Tommy bent down to place a lock of his father's hair in the ground near Drago's parents' tomb in Igrane.

Klara was Drago's "Marijana," and, yes, the wait was worth it.

Klara departed Dubrovnik as a teenager in 1957, leaving behind her family, constricted and tormented by Communism, for an uncertain future.

She and Drago created a magical life together that impacted thousands of employees and patrons, building an empire of restaurants that now is known across the world: in Old Town Dubrovnik, people walk the streets wearing Drago's baseball caps.

Klara and Drago didn't become the beacons of American freedom and success simply by selling good food. They did it by spreading

Klara and Drago were lovebirds 'til the end.

their love, helping their neighbor, never meeting a stranger, and doing the right thing when no one was looking, virtues they carried with them from the land of their birth and honed in their land of opportunity.

"It just shows you what you can do with hard work," said Mike Rodrigue, owner of Acme Oyster House. "Both Klara and Drago basically had their property taken. They were just forced out of their home country. And, now, to see the empire that was built on hard work and long hours—that just doesn't happen by accident."

"Some people call it karma," said Drago's kitchen expediter José Rodriguez. "I'm a Bible nerd, so I believe it this way, 'You sow and you reap.' It's reaping and sowing. You give and you receive. You share love, and you share grace, and it comes back to you."

After having firmly planted her American freedom flag in South Louisiana more than sixty years ago, Klara Buconic Cvitanovich, the woman whose fiancé purchased her wedding ring at Schwegmann's, is certain of one thing: "I am living the American dream to the fullest."

Index

Abadie, Maria, 124, 181, 198
Abbeville, Louisiana, 117, 180
Acme Oyster House, 68, 72, 86, 92, 122, 177, 179, 207
Adriatic Sea, 21, 26, 29-30, 35, 214
Albin, Jean-Luc (Maurice's Bakery), 139
Alessandrini, Franco, 210
Allen Toussaint Boulevard, 64, 86
America, 15-16, 35, 38, 43-44, 46, 67, 109, 134, 140, 152, 160, 162, 199, 203
American Automobile Association (AAA), 59
Anna Thomas, 65, 73, 84-86, 89, 91, 93
Antoine's, 113
Archbishop Rummel High School, 83
Archdiocese of New Orleans, 153
Argus, Krewe of, 35, 42, 71, 116, 139-41
Arnaud's, 113
Atlanta Falcons, 206
Aunt Katie, 26
Aunt Zela, 43-44, 46, 48, 50, 58
Austin, Texas, 119
Australia, 45
Austro-Hungarian Empire, 15

badnjak, Yule log, 208
Barataria Bay, 114
Barton Creek Country Club, 119
Batinich, Drago, 19, 38, 56, 65, 68
Batinich, Gloria Cvitanovich (Drago's sister), 19, 38-39, 45, 49, 56, 58, 64-65, 67-71, 79, 167
Batinich, Joan, 65, 69
Batinich, Mary Ann, 65, 69
Batinich, Sam, 38
Batinich, Veronica, 38
Baton Rouge, Louisiana, 100, 115, 162-63, 166, 175, 197

Belgrade, Serbia, 55, 108, 204
Bennigan's, 127
Bilich, Ben, 67
Biloxi, Mississippi, 74, 120
Blaise, Saint, 160
Blitch, David, 206
Board of Health, 82
Bossier City, Louisiana, 175
Bourbon Street, 181
Boyle, Edward, Sr., 76
Breaux Mart, 138
Brees, Drew, 205-7
Brennan, Dickie, 128
Brennan, Ralph, 174
Brennan's, 113
British Columbia, 18, 45-46, 53-54, 96
Broad Street, 67
Brother Martin High School, 60
Brown, Dale, 204
Brown, Vonnie, 204
Bryant-Denny Stadium, 185
Buconic, Antun, 26, 31
Buconic, Marija (Klara's mother), 21, 27, 30, 51, 58, 81, 150, 203
Buconic, Mira (Klara's sister), 21, 30, 44, 150
Buconic, Nada (Klara's sister), 21, 30-31, 154
Buconic, Peter (Klara's grandfather), 21, 24-25, 30
Buconic, Stjepan (Klara's father), 15, 18, 21-24, 26-27, 29-31, 33, 43-44, 50
Bud's Broiler, 179
Bukumirovich, Nebojsa, 204
Buras, Louisiana, 38, 48-49, 52, 64

Café du Monde, 113, 181
Canada, 17, 35, 45, 133

Canadian Restaurant Association, 127
Canal Street, 50, 59, 61-62, 72-73, 86, 92, 200
Caravan Tours, 62
Caribbean, 100
Carmel, California, 207
Cassibry, Fred, 77
Castro, Fidel, 76
Catherine of Siena, Saint, 188
Catholic Community Foundation, 161
Causeway, 73
Central Grocery, 113
cevapcici, 109-10
charbroiled oysters, 17, 79, 112-13, 116-24, 130, 152, 179, 192, 200, 205, 207
Chase, Leah, 113, 190
Cherbourg, France, 15, 44, 46
Chicago, Illinois, 56, 108, 203
Chris' Steak House, 67
Claiborne Avenue, 90
Clancy's, 113
Clarence, 65
Clement of Rome, Saint, 134, 144, 149, 188, 190
Cleveland, Flo, 59-60
Cleveland, Ohio, 35
Clinton, Hillary, 159
Cloutier, Dr., 98
Coca-Cola Refreshments, 121
Collin, Richard H., 78-79, 106-09
Commander's Palace, 113, 196, 205
Communist oppression, 35
Communists, 18
Copeland, Al, Jr., 179
coroner, 104
Crazy Johnny's Steak House, 128
Croatia, 15, 33, 35, 38-39, 41, 46, 48, 54, 59-61, 101, 140, 143, 151-52, 154-61, 176, 211, 214
Croatian, 16-19, 27, 35, 37-38, 41, 45-46, 51, 54, 56, 60, 67, 74, 81, 85, 96, 101, 108, 110-11, 126, 132, 136-38, 150-52, 154-55, 159, 161-62, 179, 201-4, 214
Cuba, 76
Cvitanovic', Bara, 35, 74
Cvitanovic', Dragutin, 35, 41
Cvitanovich, Andrew, 74-75
Cvitanovich, Barbara, 64
Cvitanovich, Callie, 140
Cvitanovich, David, Jr., 38-39, 64, 71, 75, 81, 120-21, 162

Cvitanovich, David, Sr., 38, 45, 49, 64
Cvitanovich, Dominic, 75
Cvitanovich, Drago, 16-20, 33-42, 44-46, 48-58, 60-62, 64-96, 99-103, 106-9, 111, 115-22, 124-49, 151, 153-59, 161-70, 175-77, 179-81, 184-89, 191, 197, 201, 203-4, 208-17
Cvitanovich, Gerry, 17, 33, 55, 57, 60, 64-65, 67-69, 71-72, 80, 94-105, 111, 118, 125-26, 130-31, 134-35, 137, 140-42, 144-48, 151, 156, 159, 162, 167, 170, 175-76, 189, 201, 210, 212, 214, 216
Cvitanovich, Heidi, 144-45, 175
Cvitanovich, Josh, 214
Cvitanovich, Klara Buconic, 15-35, 37, 39, 41-69, 72-78, 81, 84-88, 90-102, 105-11, 114-16, 119, 126-27, 129-32, 134, 136-40, 142-43, 145-47, 150-57, 159-62, 164, 167-68, 170, 172, 175-76, 180-89, 192-94, 197, 201, 203-5, 211, 217-18
Cvitanovich, Maddie, 140, 179
Cvitanovich, Mary, 38
Cvitanovich, Maya, 103
Cvitanovich, Tommy, 17, 19, 54-55, 57, 60-61, 64-65, 67-69, 71-74, 77, 79-84, 88, 89, 93-95, 104, 110-11, 113-31, 134, 136-43, 147-49, 156, 159, 162-92, 194-98, 200-1, 204-7, 212, 214, 217
Czechoslovakia, 26

D. H. Holmes, 61-63, 69, 72, 78, 92, 97-98
Dalmatia, 21, 39, 107
Dayton Peace Agreement, 159
Decatur Street, 199
Delgado Community College, 60
DeViney, Bob, 116, 139, 206
Disney World, 111-12
Donlic, Edin, 157
Donnell, Doug, 101
Dooky Chase Restaurant, 113, 191
Dragljane, Yugoslavia, 26
Drago's Restaurant (original on Harrison Avenue), 19, 38, 56, 58, 64, 69, 79
Dubrovnik, 18, 21, 24, 26-31, 33-35, 43-44, 46, 59, 63, 101, 108, 150-51, 154-57, 160-61, 163, 217
Dusanka (chef), 108

Index

Earl K. Long Hospital, 100
East Jefferson General Hospital, 100, 144, 211
Eastwood, Clint, 207
Egypt, 39
Eighty-second Airborne Division, 152
Eiserloh, Mark, 198
Elizabeth, Queen, 75
Ella Brennan Lifetime Achievement Award, 212
Emerald Street, 64
Emeril's, 196
English as a Second Language (ESL), 54
English Turn, 206
Erath, Louisiana, 180
Esposito, Eddie, 74, 141, 147, 151
Europe, 62, 63, 100, 143-44, 152

Fat City, 106, 109, 163, 177
Feed My Sheep, 152, 157
Fertel, Ruth, 67, 164-65, 173-75
figs, 67
First Communion, 27
Fish, Nancy, 214
FOCUS television, 152
Foley, Mr., 60
Francis (pope), 153
Franciscan Seminary, 37
Frazer River, 18
freedom, 15, 30, 33-34, 42, 76-77, 160-161, 217-218
French Quarter Fest, 118
Funk, Jim, 128

Galatoire's, 113, 181, 196, 205
Gallier Hall, 188
Galveston Bay, 119
Game of Thrones, 30
Gelpi, David, 19
Gentilich, Johnny, 188
Germans, 18, 21, 23-34, 26, 29-30, 39
Germany, 35, 45, 151, 155
Gernon Brown Playground, 94
Gimnazija (Dubrovnik high school), 44
Gourmet Butcher Block, 166
Graves' disease, 97
Grodsky, Mel, 170

Hannan, Philip, 152-3, 155, 167-8
Hardy Amies, 146
Harrison Avenue, 17, 19, 38, 56, 64, 69, 71-72, 79, 167-68
Hawaii, 100-101

Hawkins, Mary Ann, 150
Heimlich maneuver, 104
Hennesy, C. Allen, 76
Hessmer Farms, 73
Hitler, 39
Hocevar, Nada, 46
Hoss, Mike, 141, 159
Hudson River, 44, 48
Hurricane Betsy, 64, 67, 164
Hurricane Ida, 186-87
Hurricane Katrina, 16-19, 71, 91, 140, 162-74, 184, 187-88, 190-91, 204
Hurricane Laura, 187
Hynes Elementary School, 62, 64

Iberville Housing Project, 86
Iberville Street, 72
Igrane, Croatia, 35, 39, 45, 53, 214

Jackson Square, 118, 123, 199
Jackson, Mississippi, 175
Jefferson Parish, 73, 104, 116, 166-77
Jenkins, Larry, 88
Jenkins, Mama Ruth, 65, 73, 78, 84-86, 88-89, 91, 93
Jessie, 73
Jesuit High School, 97
John Paul II, Saint, 161
Jolie, Angelina, 207
Jones, Nelson, 76
Jovanovich, Zoran, 204

K&B, 96, 98, 105
Kajun Kettle Foods, 166
Katharine Drexel, Saint, 152
Kelly, Grace, 44
King, Don, 35
King's Landing, 30, 34
Klagenfurt, Austria, 151
Krafft, Joseph, 210, 212
Kraft Foods, 166
Krauss Department Store, 86
Kurtich, Eddie, 81

La Fete, 118
Lafayette, Louisiana, 175
Lafitte Housing Project, 86
Lagasse, Emeril, 174
Lahasky, Janet, 180
Lahasky, Joshua, 180
Lahasky, Ronnie, 117, 128, 135, 180-83, 197

Lake Charles, Louisiana, 175, 187
Lake Pontchartrain, 64, 73
Lakeshore, 64
Lakeside Seafood Restaurant, 77-79, 92, 106
Lakeside Shopping Center, 69, 73, 78, 93, 170
Lakeview, 16-17, 38-39, 56, 58, 62, 65, 67, 71-73, 77-80, 86, 97, 106, 167-69, 193
Landry's, 56, 69
Latin, 37
L'Auberge Casino Resort, 175
Laundromat, 74, 80
Leach, Ryan, 185-86
Legendre (Drago's staff), 65, 73, 86-87
Lepoglava prison, 29
Lillooet Ranges, 54
Little Rock, Arkansas, 61
London, England 63, 146
Louisiana Alcoholic Beverage Control Board, 76
Louisiana Hospitality Foundation, 212
Louisiana Lottery, 138
Louisiana Orange Festival, 38
Louisiana Restaurant Association (LRA), 127
Louisiana Secretary of State, 77
Louisiana State University School of Medicine, 99
Loupe, Bob, 73
Lovrijenac, Fort (Fort of St. Lawrence), 30
Lower Ninth Ward, 16
Lucky Dogs, 179
Lulich Brothers Orange Winery, 38, 52
Lulich, A. J., 38, 41, 52, 71, 128, 136, 138, 146-47, 187, 198, 201
Lulich, Ante, 38
Lulich, Mary Cvitanovich, 38, 45, 49
Lusco, Thomas, 115

Mahoney, Bobby, 75, 120
Mahoney, Mary Cvitanovich, 74-75, 120
Manale's, 113
Manhattan, New York, 44
Maravich, 203
Maravich, Press, 203
Marble Hall Saloon, 188
Mardi Gras, 48-50, 116, 139-41
Maric, Nada Buconic, 30
"Marijana," 216-17
Marine Corps, 185-86
Mary Mahoney's Old French House Restaurant, 74, 120, 180

Matesich, Johnny, 140, 188-9
Matulich, Chris, 67
Maurice's Bakery, 139
Mayo Clinic (Rochester, Minnesota), 98-100
McKnight, Freddie, 19, 84, 88-91, 163-64, 195
Meadows-Draughon Business College, 59
Medjugorje, 152-54, 156
Memphis Street, 64
Mercy Hospital, 97
Messina's, 206
Metairie, 17-18, 34-35, 73, 69, 75, 77-79, 86, 92-93, 96, 101, 103, 106, 119, 124, 136, 143-44, 149-50, 154, 157, 163, 166, 168, 170, 173, 175, 179, 184, 187, 193, 200, 207
Meyer, Conrad, III, 74
Meyer, Tony, 200-201
Michael's Steakhouse, 99
Mickelson, Phil, 206
Mildred, 65, 73, 86
Mississippi Gulf Coast, 119
Mistich, Glenn, 166
Monaco, 44
Monte Carlo, 63
Montes de Oca, Brittney, 132, 134, 144-45, 211
Monument to the Immigrant, 210
Morovich, Jelka and Violet, 48, 56
Morovich, Maria, 38
Mount Sinai, 39
muckalica, 109
Mule, Hubie and Kay, 154
Munich, 151, 155
musaka, 109-10
Mussolini, Benito, 39

Nanaimo, Vancouver Island, 45
Natalina, Sister, 27
National Federation of Croatian Americans, 159
National Restaurant Association (NRA), 127, 173
Netherlands, 60
New Jersey, 43-44, 46, 48, 50
New Orleans Hilton Riverside Hotel, 120, 123, 175, 184, 206
New Orleans Saints, 175, 199
New Orleans, Louisiana, 16-19, 38, 48-50, 52, 56, 58, 60, 63, 64-65, 67, 69, 74, 76, 78-79, 81, 84, 86, 91, 96, 98-99, 102, 107, 110, 113, 116, 120, 122,

126, 128, 141-42, 151-53, 155-56, 159, 162, 164-65, 167-68, 170, 172-73, 175-79, 180-81, 184, 187-88, 191, 196, 199, 200, 203, 205-6, 212
New Zealand, 38, 45
Nicaud, Albert, 38, 83, 87, 111-12, 117-18, 126, 133-34, 136-38, 148, 177, 186, 212-13, 216
NOLA No-Call, 199-201
North Arnoult Road, 73

O'Neal, Shaquille, 207
Occhipinti, Vera Buconic, 19, 60, 62, 142, 176-77
Ochsner, 104
Only in America, 35, 42
Orleans Avenue Canal, 64
Ošlje, Yugoslavia, 21, 26-27, 29-30
Our Lady of Good Harbor Catholic Church (Buras, Louisiana), 48
Oysters Mosca, 113
Oysters, 41, 79, 82-83, 107, 113

Paris, France 63, 86, 159
Pass Christian, Mississippi, 119
Passons, Ron, 116, 139
Payroll Protection Program (PPP), 186
Payton, Sean, 199, 204, 207
Pelican Homestead, 74
Philip Neri, Saint, 188
Pierre, Ron, Saint, 184-87
pileci paprikas, 110
Pitt, Brad, 207
Plaquemines Parish, 38, 81-82
platonic dish, 107, 109
Podgora, Yugoslavia, 26
Pope John Paul II Award, 161
Popich, Ivana, 19, 135, 207
Porter Stevens, 170
POSitouch (point-of-sale system), 111, 195
Prudhomme, Paul, 113, 120
punjena lignje, 109

Queen Mary, 15-16, 44, 46

Rainier, Prince, 44
raznici, 109, 110
Reader's Digest, 96, 98, 105
Red Danice Hrvatske, 159
Republic Beverage, 166
Rex, 50
riblja marinada, 109

Robert E. Lee Theater, 64
Robey-Coleman, Nickell, 199
Rodrigue, Mike, 122, 207
Rodriguez, Frank, 143
Rodriguez, José, 143-44, 184, 197
Rome, Italy, 63, 152-53
Rose Bowl, 201
Russia, 32
Ruth's Chris Steak House, 67, 164, 173

Safety Finance, 74
Scalia, Antonin, 207
Schellang, Evie, 150
Schwegmann's, 50, 81, 218
Seattle, Washington, 53
Second Harvest Food Bank of Greater New Orleans and Acadiana, 188
Serbia, 15, 29
Seton Portage, 54
Seventeenth Street Canal, 16
Shushan Brothers, 81
sign of the cross, 101
Simic, Joseph, 56
Singh, Vijay, 206
Sinj, Croatia, 37
Sisters of the Blessed Sacrament, 152
Slade, Dr., 96
Slovenia, 39, 41, 151
Solomon (Drago's staff), 73, 86
Spears, Britney, 207
Spenja (baker), 18
Spokane, Washington, 56
SS Constitution, 43, 101
St. Anthony of Padua, 56
St. Dominic Catholic Church, 16-17, 19-20, 71, 78, 167-70
St. Louis Cathedral, 118, 181, 185
States-Item, 79, 106
Steven Seagal, 71
Ston, Yugoslavia, 27, 41
Stuart Prep, 96
Stupa, Yugoslavia, 15, 21-22, 24, 27, 30, 41, 152, 156-57
Super Bowl, 120, 124, 130, 199

Talbot, Kirk, 179
Tampax, 37
Terrebonne Parish, 114
Tesanovic, Deša, 155-57, 161
Tesanovic, Sandi, 155-56
Thomas, Anna, 65, 73, 84-89, 91, 93
Times-Picayune, 118, 121, 151, 189

Tito, Josip Broz, 15, 33-34
Tivoli Hotel, 75
Toronto, Canada, 45
Trebinje (Yugoslavian jail), 24
Truman, Harry, 43
Trumanova jaja, 43
Tucepi, Croatia, 45
Tudjman, Franjo, 159
Tulane University, 99, 125
Tuscaloosa, Alabama, 185

Underground Gourmet, 79, 106-9
United Slavonian Benevolent Association (USBA), 204
University of New Orleans, 83

Vancouver Island, 45
Vancouver, Canada, 18, 45, 54, 56, 96
Vinovich, Bill, 201
Voice of America, 33

Walmart, 50
Warehouse District, 130, 175
Warren Easton High School, 59
Weigand, Rocky, 121, 128-31, 177, 179, 187
Werlein's, 72

Whitfield, Preston, 163
Who Dat Nation, 199
Whole Foods, 166
Wildlife and Fisheries, 82
Willie Mae's, 113
Winn-Dixie, 64
Woldenberg Park, 210
Worden, Billy, Jr., 63, 92
Worden, W. H., Sr., 61, 63, 98
World Cup, 144, 201
World War II, 15, 18, 21, 35, 38-39, 41, 43, 86, 133, 135, 152, 155

Xavier University of Louisiana, 152
Yankee Stadium, 162
Yugoslav-American Club, 126
Yugoslavia, 15, 18, 21, 26-27, 32-35, 38-39, 41, 43-45, 54, 63, 134, 151-52, 155, 159-60, 181, 201, 204
Yugoslavian partisans, 24

Zagreb, Croatia, 46, 161
Zagreb, University of, 37, 41, 46
Zea's Rotisserie and Grill, 166
Ziegler, Mel, 179
Zurich Classic, 206-7